the wedding planner

the wedding planner

Holly Lefevre

Bath · New York · Singapore · Hong Kong · Cologne · Delhi · Melbourne

This edition published by Parragon in 2008
Parragon
Queen Street House
4 Queen Street
Bath BA1 1HE, UK

ISBN: 978-1-4075-1903-6
Printed in China

Created and produced by the Bridgewater Book Company Ltd

*With thanks to the Clifton Photographic Company
for permission to reproduce copyright material.
www.cliftonphoto.co.uk Tel: +44 (0)117 9098985*

Contents

1

Introduction

♥ Essential Wedding Planning Rules

♥ Get Organized

♥ Resources and Information for Planning

♥ Twelve-Month Wedding Planning

   Calendar and Checklist

In one short breathtaking instance, your life changed. No longer is he just the boyfriend—he is your fiancé. You are engaged! And terrified… and excited… and overwhelmed. From the moment he proposed, your mind has not stopped— call Mom, call best friend, call caterer, call hotel, call band, call florist. Okay, the first two tasks were easy, but where do you start with the rest?

Essential Wedding Planning Rules

Planning a wedding can be fun, but it is a lot of work. For some brides, it becomes a second job, for others it takes over their lives. So, how will you juggle the roles of working woman and bride-to-be? Information and organization will ensure your success. Following this set of rules will help you make decisions, stay on budget, and avoid bridal overload:

BE DOLLAR WISE Determine your priorities up front. What do you want? What does your fiancé want? What can you afford? What are you willing to do without? Where is the money coming from? Put the budget down in writing and track it.

BE OPEN Learn from the mistakes and triumphs of friends, family, and co-workers. Ask them what they did right and what they would do differently.

BE SMART Don't get carried away in the wonderful craziness of wedding planning and fall prey to high-pressure sales tactics and too-good-to-be-true offers.

BE WILLING TO ASK FOR HELP Include the groom in the planning and delegate some responsibilities to him. And don't forget you have family and friends who can help, too. If you need additional assistance, a professional wedding planner may be your answer.

BE YOURSELF The best weddings have personal touches and are a reflection of the bride and groom. Use your creativity, interests, hobbies, and so on to add these touches.

BE RELAXED If you get frazzled or stressed during the planning, take a break and regroup. On the wedding day itself, just go with the flow. If something different happens to what you expected, the chances are only a handful of people will ever know. People are not there to judge your wedding, but to share this wonderful occasion with you.

The best weddings have touches that are a reflection of the bride and groom

Introduction

Get Organized

★ UPON ENGAGEMENT

As you make your way through the wedding planning process, it is important to keep accurate and thorough records. The most important aspect of any organizational system is to make sure it works with your lifestyle and fits into your current daily routine. Review the information below and use the suggestions to help you to develop your own system for keeping your wedding planning progress organized and easily at hand.

The perfect on-the-go system is a wedding binder. A substantial three-ring binder filled with sheet protectors not only provides enough space to organize important papers, compile actual samples of a vendor's work (for example, wedding programs, photographs, and calligraphy styles), but it can also be updated continually and all of your information is readily accessible. (Be sure to create separate, stay-at-home files to keep original copies of vendor contracts safe: a good old-fashioned filing system works well. You can set one up in an already existing file cabinet at your home or purchase a portable file system at an office supply store.)

A wedding binder is the perfect on-the-go system for organizing information

If the computer is a part of your daily life, it is logical to use it to help to organize your wedding details. You can use spreadsheets to keep track of guest lists and budget matters. Email has made it very easy to communicate with friends, family, and suppliers at all times of the day or night. It is especially useful for connecting with wedding vendors as you have written records of conversations. You may want to set up a separate (free) email account for your wedding correspondence and give this address to vendors. This not only keeps your information organized and all in one location, but also on those days that you do not feel like planning, you do not have to check that email.

Once you have established your organizational system, set aside time each week to refresh it. Pick a date that is typically less busy, an evening at the weekend, perhaps. File anything that has not been filed, review information from the past week, and make a list of what you want or need to accomplish for the upcoming week.

Resources and Information for Planning

For very little effort you have access to a plethora of information on wedding design, planning, etiquette—in fact, wedding everything! Start a system for keeping fabric swatches, magazine tearsheets, and photos that reflect your ideas and style. Look for information everywhere, including the following readily available resources:

BRIDAL EXPOS There are vendors from every category who are available and ready to answer your questions. You can watch fashion shows to see the latest gowns, tuxedos, and bridesmaids' dresses.

WEDDING LIBRARIES AND SHOWROOMS Operating like a small version of a bridal show, libraries and showrooms offer couples an opportunity to view a variety of vendors in the comfort of their showrooms.

THE INTERNET Many websites are affiliated with large bridal magazines, and offer everything from details of local vendors to accessories and supplies. There are also chat rooms where brides can review and critique wedding vendors and discuss their personal planning.

PROFESSIONAL ASSOCIATIONS These groups often provide a database that represents a good starting point for finding information and particular types of vendors, but you must still do your research; while belonging to an association does show some commitment to one's craft, it does not always mean that the vendor is the best one for you.

PUBLICATIONS There are countless magazines and books devoted solely to gowns, cakes, flowers, or destination weddings, as well as magazines that cover the entire spectrum of wedding planning.

WEDDING PLANNER If you are using a professional wedding planner take advantage of his or her experience and connections. If you trust this person enough to assist you with your planning, you should trust their judgment on vendors and advice, too.

OTHER BRIDES One of the best (and sometimes most honest) sources for information in the wedding world is other brides. They will love to talk about their experiences and are often more than happy to share the good, bad, and ugly of locations, vendors, and planning secrets.

Probably one of the best and most honest sources of information is other brides

Twelve-Month Wedding Planning Calendar and Checklist

This calendar includes the essential elements of wedding planning. Personalize the sections by crossing out items not relevant to you and color-coding the list (with highlighter markers) using a different color for bride's tasks, groom's tasks, and others, such as your mother's or bridesmaids' duties, or according to personal priority.

TWELVE MONTHS PLUS

- [x] Select and purchase engagement ring
- [x] Announce the engagement
- [x] Set the date
- [x] Attend engagement party
- [x] Hire a wedding planner
- [ ] Draft a preliminary guest list
- [x] Draft a budget
- [x] Begin bridal registry
- [x] Determine the style and formality of the wedding
- [x] Research and select ceremony site
- [x] Research and select reception location
- [x] Research wedding vendors

TEN TO TWELVE MONTHS

- [x] Select wedding party
- [x] Interview and select vendors:
  - [x] Caterer (if necessary)
  - [x] Photographer
  - [ ] Videographer/cinematographer
  - [x] Entertainment/music
  - [ ] Florist/event designer
- [x] Shop for wedding gown
- [x] Upon hiring photographer, schedule an engagement session

EIGHT TO TEN MONTHS

- [x] Purchase wedding insurance
- [x] Order wedding gown
- [x] Organize accommodation and transportation for out-of-town guests

- [x] Select and order save-the-date cards
- [ ] Organize accommodation for the wedding night (and night before)
- [ ] Interview and select vendors:
  - [x] Rentals equipment
  - [ ] Specialty rentals
  - [ ] Lighting
  - [x] Officiant (if you are not marrying in a house of worship)
- [x] Research wedding invitations
- [ ] Research honeymoon, for example passport requirements

SIX TO EIGHT MONTHS

- [x] Begin planning ceremony
- [ ] Begin planning reception
- [x] Plan the rehearsal dinner
- [ ] Plan pre-wedding and post-wedding parties
- [ ] Begin dance lessons (if necessary)
- [ ] Finalize any remaining vendor commitments:
  - [x] Hair stylist for wedding day
  - [ ] Makeup stylist for wedding day
  - [x] Valet parking attendants (if necessary)
  - [x] Pastry chef/select wedding cake
- [x] Mail save-the-date cards
- [ ] Research other stationery needs (menu cards, place cards, ceremony programs)
- [x] Order bridesmaids' dresses
- [ ] Help mothers shop for their attire

- [x] Select formalwear for the groom, groomsmen, and fathers
- [x] Research favor options
- [ ] Plan and book honeymoon
- [ ] Get passports (if necessary)

FOUR TO SIX MONTHS

- [x] Finalize guest list
- [x] Order wedding invitations and announcements
- [x] Order invitations for rehearsal dinner, and pre-/post-wedding parties
- [x] Determine reception menu
- [x] Hire calligrapher for invitations and place cards
- [ ] Select wedding-day transportation
- [ ] Shop for wedding bands
- [ ] Shop for bridal accessories (headpiece/veil, lingerie, jewelry, and so on)
- [ ] Shop for bridesmaids' accessories (jewelry, shoes, purses)
- [x] Research ideas for welcome gifts
- [ ] Develop a preliminary wedding-day timeline/schedule

THREE MONTHS

- [ ] Address and assemble invitations
- [ ] Research marriage license requirements
- [ ] Confirm delivery dates on wedding gown and bridesmaids' dresses
- [ ] Compile music list for reception entertainment

- [ ] Finalize ceremony details and music selections
- [ ] Begin creating ceremony program and order
- [ ] Prepare shoot list for videographer and photographer
- [ ] Shop for attendants' thank you gifts
- [ ] Make arrangements for preserving bridal bouquet
- [ ] Make arrangements for preserving bridal gown

TWO MONTHS

- [ ] Mail invitations
- [ ] Finalize rehearsal dinner plans and send out invitations
- [ ] Attend dress fittings/alterations
- [ ] Confirm with bridesmaids that they have purchased lingerie and shoes, and have scheduled/attended their dress fitting
- [ ] Schedule wedding day hair and makeup preview/trial
- [ ] Complete wedding-day timeline/schedule
- [ ] Finalize ceremony program
- [ ] Prepare wedding announcement for newspaper
- [ ] Attend wedding showers
- [ ] Begin collecting wedding accessories
- [ ] Schedule final beauty/grooming appointments for the week of wedding: haircut and/or color, manicure/pedicure, massage, tanning, waxing

ONE MONTH

- [ ] Obtain marriage license
- [ ] Finalize itinerary with vendors and ceremony/reception locations
- [ ] Begin making seating plan for reception dinner
- [ ] Pick up wedding bands
- [ ] Schedule final gown fittings and date

to pick up finished and pressed wedding gown
- [ ] Call guests who have not responded to invitation
- [ ] Start on/complete thank you notes for any wedding gifts already received
- [ ] Break in your wedding shoes
- [ ] Prepare welcome gifts (excluding perishable items)

TWO WEEKS

- [ ] Confirm final guest count to caterer/reception location
- [ ] Confirm rehearsal dinner guest count
- [ ] Begin packing for honeymoon
- [ ] Begin making final payments to vendors (payments due from this point up to wedding day)
- [ ] Finalize seating plan and send seating/place cards to calligrapher
- [ ] Prepare an "emergency kit" for wedding-day mishaps

ONE WEEK

- [ ] Pick up gown—try it on at the dressmaker's for final fit, and do not try it on again at home
- [ ] Attend final grooming/beauty appointments
- [ ] Call/email venues and all vendors to finalize arrangements, delivery times, and any other details
- [ ] Attend bachelor/bachelorette parties
- [ ] Finalize packing for honeymoon
- [ ] Arrange to have your mail stopped during your honeymoon
- [ ] Attend bridal luncheon

TWO TO THREE DAYS

- [ ] Prepare tips for vendors
- [ ] Drop off wedding accessories at venue or deliver to wedding planner
- [ ] Deliver welcome gifts to hotels

- [ ] Pack a bag for the wedding day
- [ ] Pick up tuxedos for groom, groomsmen, and fathers. Try on tuxedos—confirm all articles of clothing and accessories have been supplied
- [ ] Cut checks for remaining vendor payments

ONE DAY TO GO

- [ ] Attend ceremony rehearsal
- [ ] Distribute the wedding-day itinerary to all parents, attendants, and other involved parties
- [ ] Hand over remaining accessories to wedding planner, church coordinator, or other organizer
- [ ] Attend rehearsal dinner
- [ ] Present attendants with their gifts at the rehearsal dinner
- [ ] Go to bed early so you will be well rested for the amazing day that lies ahead of you

THE WEDDING DAY

- [ ] Give vendor tips and payments to planner or best man for distribution
- [ ] Get beautiful
- [ ] Get dressed
- [ ] Marry the man you love and have a great day!

POST WEDDING

- [ ] Leave for honeymoon
- [ ] Have bouquet sent for preservation
- [ ] Send gown for cleaning and preservation
- [ ] Complete and mail thank you cards
- [ ] Thank your parents and attendants (by phone call and/or note)
- [ ] Thank your vendors (by phone call and/or note)
- [ ] Change name

The
Engagement

2

- ♥ The Engagement Ring
- ♥ Set the Wedding Date
- ♥ Announce Your Engagement
- ♥ Bridal Gift Registry

Y ou may have been presented with an engagement ring when your loved one asked you to marry him. Or it may be that your fiancé wants you to choose one together. You should do so prior to making an official engagement announcement. Apart from selecting a wedding date, this is the time to prepare your bridal gift registry and to plan the first of many wonderful parties.

The Engagement Ring

★ PRIOR TO OFFICIAL ENGAGEMENT ANNOUNCEMENT

Your engagement ring is probably one of the most expensive, exquisite, and sentimental pieces of jewelry you will ever own. Ring shopping can be nerve-wracking, as you prepare to spend big money on a diamond. Get references from friends and family for reputable jewelers.

Tip Don't forget to ask the jeweler for instructions on the proper care of the ring. Many jewelers will allow you to bring the ring in for regular checkups and cleaning. Finally, be sure to contact your insurance agent to obtain additional insurance on the engagement ring.

Before you head to the jewelers, acquaint yourself with the finer points of diamonds, and most importantly the "4 Cs":

♥ Carat: the overall weight of a diamond
♥ Cut: the shape, cut, or proportions of the stone
♥ Clarity: a measure of the amount and variety of flaws in a diamond
♥ Color: a measure of the color of the stone. A "perfect" diamond is colorless

Together the 4 Cs determine the overall value and beauty of any particular diamond. The Internet is a good place to study up on the finer points of the 4 Cs before going to choose your ring. Once you make your decision, you should expect to get a diamond-grading report. You should also have the ring's 4 Cs recorded on your invoice/bill of sale.

Set the Wedding Date

Choosing a date is the first major step in your planning, as it sets the timeline and basic framework for your wedding. Therefore it is an important decision that requires some careful thought and investigation. In conjunction with other aspects of wedding planning, the date can also influence the overall style and formality of the wedding. Unless a particular date holds special significance, it is best to determine a general timeframe for the wedding—a month or a season—rather than settling on a particular date. This allows you more leeway when it comes to selecting wedding locations.

When you are looking at a date/dates, consider the following circumstances and situations that could impact on your wedding planning:

- If you are planning to marry in a house of worship, you need to determine availability. Many religious institutions have restrictions for performing marriage ceremonies at particular times of the year—during high holidays, for instance. Many also have restrictions on timing—for example, confession and mass in the Catholic Church rule out certain times of the day and Sundays altogether.

- You should also ask whether any special events organized by others are scheduled for that location which may coincide with your plans for that date.

- Local events such as fairs, festivals, and marathons can wreak havoc with your wedding plans because of the crowds they attract. Check with the local City Hall, Chamber of Commerce, and/or Parks and Recreation Department for event dates that may conflict. Much of this information is also posted on their websites.

- Think about the climate where you plan to marry, the season, and the type of wedding you would like to have: garden weddings in January are a risky business.

- Planning a wedding during your busiest period at work or school may pose problems. Will you be able to take the time off you need? How will you finalize all the details when you are swamped with work?

- Prime locations book anywhere between 12 and 18 months in advance, so there is always the possibility that your first choice for a date may already be allocated to someone else.

- Saturday—whether the morning, afternoon, or the evening—is the most popular day of the week and books quickly throughout the year. Friday evenings and Sundays are also great options but again, these are popular choices.

Announce Your Engagement

As a newly engaged woman, you probably cannot wait to call your family and friends and share your good news. In a perfect world, couples should wait until they can gather their families and make the announcement simultaneously. However, it is increasingly likely that families and friends are spread far and wide over states, countries, even continents, so this is not always possible.

When it is time to announce your engagement, if you cannot do it in person, be sure to make the really important phone calls first: your parents, his parents, grandparents, siblings, and very close relatives. Then let close friends (those who will definitely be invited to the wedding) know. While it may not be considered (strictly) proper etiquette, mass emails and text messages will get the news quickly to your friends and some relatives, though if you decide to do this you should still call your parents and grandparents first.

Public Announcements

A printed piece in the local paper, your hometown newspaper (if that is different), the newspaper local to where your parents reside, and alumni publications also spreads the news. Call each publication to obtain a copy of the publication guidelines. The following is typical information published in an announcement:

- ♥ Bride's information: full name, hometown of the bride, parents of the bride.
- ♥ Groom's information: full name, hometown of the groom, parents of the groom.
- ♥ General location: city, state, or country where wedding will take place.
- ♥ Date: if some arrangements have been confirmed you may wish to include a month or season and the year, but do not include the specific date.
- ♥ Optional information may include: occupation of bride/groom, college of bride/groom, names of maid/matron of honor, best man, and wedding party.

Here is a sample of a traditional published engagement announcement issued by the bride's parents. The wording may be altered to reflect numerous situations such as the announcement being issued by the groom's parents, by the bride and groom themselves, or any combination of single or step parents:

Mr. and Mrs. Steven Jones of Monterey announce the engagement of their daughter, Sophia Ann, to Mr. Joseph Smith, son of Mr. and Mrs. Randall Smith of San Francisco. The couple is planning a wedding next Spring in Napa Valley.

Finally, printed engagement announcements are also an option for spreading the news. Printed announcements are similar in style to a wedding invitation, and should also reflect the formality and style of the wedding. Typical wording for an engagement announcement might be:

Mr. and Mrs. (NAMES OF PARENTS OF THE BRIDE)
are pleased to announce the engagement of their daughter, (INSERT NAME)
to (INSERT GROOM NAME), *son of* (NAMES OF PARENTS OF GROOM)
The wedding will take place on (INSERT MONTH/YEAR) *in* (INSERT CITY AND STATE)
Invitation to follow

Bridal Gift Registry

★ UPON ENGAGEMENT

Major department stores, chain retailers, specialty stores, travel agents, home improvement stores, and mortgage companies offer bridal gift registry options. Or you can set up a registry with your preferred charity and ask guests to make a donation in lieu of gifts. Keep in mind that although a gift registry is convenient for everyone, expect to receive items that are not on the list, and be gracious about it. You should begin compiling a gift registry early in the planning, prior to the engagement party. You may continue to update and alter the list for a few months, but your registry should be complete before the bridal showers begin. To get started, select one to three stores or companies you would like to register with. Often, you can register and research registries online or pick up detailed information packets in the store. A bridal gift registry should include a selection of diverse items in different price ranges to appeal to all guests and all budgets.

You can tell guests about your bridal gift registry through word of mouth (parents, wedding party, close friends), enclosures with your bridal shower invitations, or on your wedding website. Do not include bridal gift registry information with the wedding invitation, and if you would prefer to receive money, again let people know through word of mouth.

Although a gift registry is convenient, expect to receive items that are not on the list

Gift Registry Information

STORE:

CONTACT:

PHONE:

EMAIL:

FAX:

SPECIAL INSTRUCTIONS/DETAILS:

STORE:

CONTACT:

PHONE:

EMAIL:

FAX:

SPECIAL INSTRUCTIONS/DETAILS:

STORE:

CONTACT:

PHONE:

EMAIL:

FAX:

SPECIAL INSTRUCTIONS/DETAILS:

STORE:

CONTACT:

PHONE:

EMAIL:

FAX:

SPECIAL INSTRUCTIONS/DETAILS:

The Engagement

Getting Started

♥ Preliminary Guest List

♥ Wedding Insurance

♥ Hiring a Wedding Planner

♥ Prepare the Budget

Wedding planning can seem terribly overwhelming to an already busy bride to be. The key priorities are to prepare your guest list and to establish who is paying for the wedding. If you are intending to hire a professional wedding planner to help take some of the strain out of the process it is wise to hire one early on so that you may benefit from his or her knowledge throughout the planning.

Preliminary Guest List
★ UPON ENGAGEMENT

Your guest list will normally start with members of your joint immediate family, close relatives, and close personal and family friends. Often the list includes bosses, co-workers, and other business associates. Before you can draft a budget and begin the search for a wedding location, you must know how many guests you expect to invite to your wedding, as budgetary and space constraints affect these final decisions.

Often who makes it on the guest list is dictated by who is paying for the wedding—when parents are paying, they may expect to have a large say about who is invited. The fairest way to finalize the list is to have each person create a prioritized guest list. Divide the expected number of guests between the "inviting" parties. When you merge the lists, obviously guests' names that appear on more than one list are "in." From there on, let the negotiating begin.

Some questions to assist you in establishing guest list guidelines are:
- Will single guests be allowed to invite a guest?
- Will it need to be a long-term boyfriend/girlfriend?
- Will casual dates be included?
- Will children be invited to the wedding?
- What is the cut-off age for inviting children?
- Will co-workers be invited?
- Will distant relatives be invited?

Wedding Insurance

★ EIGHT TO TEN MONTHS

When you consider that most weddings cost as much or more than a new car, it makes perfect sense to protect your investment. Wedding insurance is a widely offered insurance program that is specifically designed for weddings and special events. Coverage can include everything from replacement costs for your wedding gown to re-creating the day should your photographer skip town with your negatives. Once you have an idea how much the wedding is going to cost, you can look into wedding insurance options. For the peace of mind it can provide, wedding insurance is an affordable and practical option for every couple.

Hiring a Wedding Planner

★ UPON ENGAGEMENT (OR AT ANY TIME)

The best wedding planners book far in advance; so look into booking one sooner rather than later. If you have already selected your venues, their representatives or managers may be able to refer you to wedding planners. If not, professional organizations also offer a referral system.

Wedding planning services vary from planner to planner.  The types of services wedding planners offer are:

- ♥ Full service planning: this is where the planner works with you from the beginning; assisting you with budgeting, finding locations and vendors, and following up on all of the details. He or she may also assist with design and style aspects of the wedding.
- ♥ Month of: for this service the planner organizes all of the work you have done into a complete wedding day itinerary. He or she comes into the picture about two months prior to the wedding day. The planner will be present at the wedding rehearsal and on the day itself to ensure everything is running smoothly and on time.
- ♥ Day of: if you hire a planner for this service, you are expected to finalize all the details and create your own itinerary. The planner will then use the information you provide to direct the rehearsal and guide you and your husband through your wedding day.

- ♥ Hourly services: if you feel you do not need a full service, and just need help in some areas, most consultants will meet with you for an hourly fee.

Wedding Planner

COMPANY:

CONTACT:

PHONE:

EMAIL:

FAX:

DEPOSIT:

FINAL PAYMENT:

SPECIAL INSTRUCTIONS:

DETAILS:

Prepare the Budget

★ UPON ENGAGEMENT

In many cultures, traditionally the bride's family was responsible for the majority of the expenses of a wedding. That is changing. Often, the bride's family, the groom's family, and the bride and groom themselves are covering the wedding expenses. You will need to establish up front who is going to contribute and how much (see below).

Keys to a Successful Budget

Talk of the "budget" can become an uncomfortable discussion about money and family politics, but it must be done. The following points will assist in preparing yourself with basic and really quite simple facts about the process, which may alleviate some of the stress:

♥ Know where the money is coming from. Have everyone involved in meeting the costs of your wedding sit down together (if possible) and get the budget in order. Ask how much each party will be contributing. If you cannot all get together, try a chat room, or emails.

♥ Determine how much money you and your fiancé can contribute—how much do you currently have and how much you think you can realistically save before the wedding. Keep track of what you are spending: it quickly adds up and before you know it you could be in over your head and find yourself paying for your wedding for a long time (at very high interest rates).

♥ Prioritize your wants and needs. Before you approach your family with your monetary requests, sit down with your fiancé and list your priorities as a couple. Make a list in order of what is most important to the two of you. When you talk to the budget contributors, you and your fiancé should present a united front on the subject of the budget.

♥ Determine where the money will go. Based on your priority list and the input of other contributors, it is time to start dividing up the money. Account for at least 50 percent of the total budget to go toward your reception costs—venue and catering. Divide the remainder among your other necessities.

Once you know your budget, you need to divide the money into the different categories of vendor services and products (the budget worksheet gives a complete list). Many factors determine how you divide these costs: the style and formality of the wedding; time of day and year; number of guests; location; and style of meal service.

♥ Compare your budget with the actual price of goods and services. Calling around, surfing the Internet, or attending a bridal show will also provide some vendor pricing information. You may also want to ask other brides about the "average" price of various services (most are willing to share), or engage a wedding planner on an hourly basis to get your budget started.

♥ Expect to go over budget (almost everyone does). Mostly you will not begrudge it, especially if you get the perfect photographer. Allot 5–10 percent of your budget to an emergency or miscellaneous category to cover unexpected items.

Budget Worksheet

ESTIMATED BUDGET: ....

FINAL BUDGET: ....

		ESTIMATE	ACTUAL	DEPOSIT	BALANCE	DUE DATE
BRIDE	GOWN					
	VEIL/HEADPIECE					
	LINGERIE/HOSIERY					
	SHOES					
	JEWELRY					
	GOWN PRESERVATION					
	OTHER					
GROOM	TUXEDO					
	SHOES					
	ACCESSORIES					
	OTHER					
BRIDAL BEAUTY	HAIR STYLIST					
	MAKEUP STYLIST					
	HAIR CUT/COLOR					
	FACIALS/WAXING					
	OTHER					
CEREMONY	SITE RENTAL FEE					
	ADDITIONAL SECURITY DEPOSIT					
	OFFICIANT FEE/DONATION					
	OTHER					
DECOR	LIGHTING					
	SPECIALITY RENTALS					
	SPECIALITY LINENS					

		ESTIMATE	ACTUAL	DEPOSIT	BALANCE	DUE DATE
FLOWERS	PERSONAL FLOWERS					
	CEREMONY					
	RECEPTION					
	BOUQUET PRESERVATION					
TRANSPORT	LIMOUSINE/CARRIAGE					
	VALET PARKING					
	SHUTTLES					
PHOTOGRAPHY	ENGAGEMENT PHOTOS					
	FORMAL PORTRAIT SESSION					
	WEDDING DAY					
	OTHER					
RECEPTION (ON-SITE CATERING)	SITE RENTAL FEE					
	ADDITIONAL SECURITY DEPOSIT					
	MEAL PRICE					
	BAR					
	CAKE					
	CHAMPAGNE TOAST					
	GRATUITY					
	COFFEE/CAPPUCCINO SERVICE					
	TAX					
	OTHER					
RECEPTION (OFF-SITE CATERING)	ALL OF THE ABOVE					
	SERVICE PERSONNEL					
	EQUIPMENT RENTALS					
	OTHER					

Getting Started

		ESTIMATE	ACTUAL	DEPOSIT	BALANCE	DUE DATE
MUSIC	CEREMONY					
	RECEPTION					
STATIONERY	INVITATIONS ENSEMBLE					
	ANNOUNCEMENTS					
	AT HOME/NAME CARDS					
	THANK YOU/INFORMAL CARDS					
	MAP/DIRECTION CARDS					
	PEW CARDS					
	POSTAGE					
HONEYMOON	TRANSPORTATION					
	ACCOMMODATION					
	DAILY FUNDS					
MISCELLANEOUS	REHEARSAL DINNER					
	VIDEOGRAPHY					
	WEDDING PLANNER					
	WEDDING RINGS					
	GIFTS (WEDDING PARTY, FAMILY)					
	DISPOSABLE CAMERAS/FILM					
	HOTEL ROOM ON WEDDING NIGHT					
	FAVORS					
	TIPS FOR VENDORS					
	ACCESSORIES					
	OTHER					
	GRAND TOTAL					

The Venue

♥ Find Your Style

♥ Selecting the Venues

From the time your engagement is announced you need to be thinking about where you want to marry. Selecting a wedding venue is an important decision that will be influenced by your lifestyle, personality, and budget. On the wedding day, it will be the addition of your personal touches and creative flourishes to the ceremony and reception that will set your wedding apart from the others.

Find Your Style
★ UPON ENGAGEMENT

Jot down some words that come to mind regarding how you feel about the style of your wedding or how you envision the event. These can include smells, colors, feelings, inspirations, poems, and songs. Then fill out the worksheet to determine your personal wedding style.

The wedding venue can dictate the formality and the overall mood of a wedding

Style Worksheet

OVERALL STYLE

☐ Casual
☐ Eclectic
☐ Informal
☐ Semi-formal
☐ Formal
☐ Very formal (black tie)

CEREMONY SETTING

☐ House of worship (church/synagogue/temple)
☐ Chapel
☐ Garden/park/beach/other outdoor location
☐ Combined ceremony/reception
☐ Courthouse/civil service

RECEPTION SETTING

☐ Hotel
☐ Garden/park/outdoor location
☐ Ocean view venue
☐ Private home/estate
☐ Banquet facility
☐ Country club/private club

WEDDING COLORS

....
....
....
....

Selecting the Venues

★ TWELVE MONTHS

The wedding venue can dictate the formality of a wedding as well as set the overall mood. Selecting a venue will also make other stylistic decisions fall into place. You may choose to take certain elements from the venue, say a rose garden, and build on that idea, incorporating a rose theme into your invitation ensemble, wedding programs, and favors.

Ceremony Venue

Before you can begin making definitive plans about your ceremony venue, you need to ask yourself certain questions to determine the essential elements of the ceremony and hence the type of venue:

- ♥ How important is religion in your ceremony?
- ♥ How important is spirituality in your ceremony?
- ♥ Do you want to be married in a house of worship? What does your fiancé want? If your opinions differ, what compromises are you willing to make?
- ♥ Are you and your fiancé of the same religious background? If you are of different religions, is a ceremony in a house of worship even an option? Is there a house of worship in your area that will accommodate this situation?
- ♥ If you do not regularly practice a religion, do the religious venues in your area allow non-members to marry there?
- ♥ Would you prefer to marry in a non-religious location? Would you prefer to have a civil ceremony?

HOUSES OF WORSHIP Traditionally weddings were held in a house of worship (such as a church, synagogue, or temple). If you choose to marry in a house of worship, there is typically an established set of standards, rules, regulations, and requirements to abide by. These "rules" cover everything from dress code to decor of the ceremony area. Most houses of worship provide an on-site wedding coordinator to guide couples through the rules and options regarding protocol and ceremony. They typically provide a standard ceremony format for you to follow. There are, however, often some means of personalizing the ceremony by way of (approved) musical selections, readings, and the addition of special ceremonies such as the unity candle or rose ceremony (see page 117). As you plan your ceremony, you will need to work within the limits and standards of the location, as well as receive approval from the coordinator and/or officiant for the final ceremony plans. (See Chapter 12 for planning the ceremony.)

NON-RELIGIOUS LOCATIONS If you choose to marry in a non-religious location such as a park, beach, hotel, or historic site, the options for creating and personalizing your wedding ceremony are numerous. Unlike weddings held in a house of worship, there is little or no restriction on the content of a ceremony held at one of these alternative locations. You and your fiancé can choose to have a ceremony that incorporates religious, spiritual, or purely legal aspects that are of significance to you—from choice of music to vows. For a ceremony held at a non-religious location, one of the most important things you need to do is hire an officiant (see Chapter 12).

The Reception Venue

There are two basic types of location: inclusive and off-premise. Finding the right reception venue requires research, detailed planning, and legwork. With your preliminary guest count and budget in mind, you are ready to begin your quest for that perfect location!

INCLUSIVE VENUES Inclusive venues include hotels, country clubs, private clubs, wedding/special event venues, and restaurants. Typically, when you book one of these venues, you are buying a "package" that includes the services of a catering manager, basic linens, china, glassware, service, use of the venue's facilities, and the cost of food and beverage. Such venues offer a range of decor, food quality, and service quality; the options can be tailored to meet your budget and taste. You may choose to upgrade linens, add lighting, and rent specialty china.

OFF-PREMISE VENUES Off-premise sites include the family home, a historic castle/mansion, a country meadow, even a public park. As a rule, the rental fee you pay for an off-premise location includes only the location. It is up to you to bring in everything from security personnel to rental equipment. Off-premise venues require highly skilled event coordination, for which you may need to hire the expertise of a professional caterer or wedding planner.

Before deciding on an off-premise venue, read the fine print of the contract and plan a reserve in your budget for emergencies, such as providing tented cover should it rain. Finally, check with local authorities for necessary permits, parking requirements, and noise restrictions.

Keep in mind your guest count and budget as you search for that perfect location

Researching Venues

It pays to check out in person the wedding reception venues that you are considering. Above all, remember your first impression—it is likely to be the same as the impression of your guests on the wedding day. Additionally, be sure to gather the appropriate information including the following:

- ☐ Take photos and ask for floor plans.
- ☐ Always check capacity.
- ☐ Ask for a copy of a contract and clarify all fees associated with having your event at that location.
- ☐ Ask about the flow of the event—where will the ceremony take place (if applicable), the cocktail hour, the dinner/reception.
- ☐ Get everything in writing. Sales and banquet managers move around to different properties, so be sure the "promised" items make it into your contract.
- ☐ At any facility or when working with a rental company, ask to see samples of their glassware, flatware, china, linen, and chairs. What you are shown in photos and brochures is not always what you get.

QUESTIONS TO ASK

- ☐ What are the contracted hours? Does that include set up and breakdown?
- ☐ Is there a cleaning fee? Is it included in the rental fee?
- ☐ Are there any overtime charges?
- ☐ Are there security charges?
- ☐ Is there a site representative who will be available on the event day? Is he/she an additional cost?
- ☐ Are there areas that we are not allowed to utilize?
- ☐ Can the caterer use the kitchen (off-premise locations)?
- ☐ How many people can be seated in the area or room?
- ☐ What is the rain contingency plan?
- ☐ What is included in the rental fee or wedding package?
- ☐ Is there a noise ordinance?
- ☐ Are there any permit fees?
- ☐ What are the parking arrangements?
- ☐ Is the site insured? Will we and our vendors need insurance?
- ☐ Are we required to use the location's preferred vendors?
- ☐ Are there an appropriate number of restrooms for our guest count?

Off-Premise Caterer
⭐ **TEN TO TWELVE MONTHS**

If you choose to hold your reception at an off-premise venue, you need to find a caterer. Ask the representative of the venue for recommendations of caterers. Things tend to go more smoothly when a caterer is familiar with a venue.

When you interview a caterer, you will be looking at their food presentation and preparation, professionalism, and, of course, their menu selection. You should also ask to taste a sampling of their food. Be very clear when you speak with them about what is included in their services. Include these specifics in your contract along with the final menu selections and prices, special requests, and establish when payments and guest counts are due.

Questions to Ask
- 💜 Do you have a portfolio of sample menus and photos of your events?
- 💜 Are you licensed and insured?
- 💜 Do you have a food specialty (Asian, Italian, family style)? If not, are you open to suggestions?
- 💜 Do you specialize in a particular style of service (buffet, plated, stations)?
- 💜 What is included in your price per person?
- 💜 Do you provide bar/beverage service? If so what is included (glasses, ice, cocktail napkins)?
- 💜 Is set up and clean up included?
- 💜 Who will be our contact during the planning? Will that person be present on the wedding day? Who will be in charge on the wedding day?
- 💜 What attire does your staff wear on the wedding day?
- 💜 How much wait staff and support staff is included/will be necessary?
- 💜 Will you assist in coordinating rentals for the day? Do you have a preferred rental company?
- 💜 Do you set up the venue (tables, chairs, linens)?

Caterer

COMPANY:

CONTACT:

PHONE:

EMAIL:

FAX:

DEPOSIT:

FINAL GUEST COUNT DUE:

FINAL PAYMENT DUE:

SPECIAL INSTRUCTIONS:

MENU DETAILS:

FAVORITE FOODS/FAMILY RECIPE/SPECIAL REQUEST:

Things tend to go more smoothly when a caterer is familiar with the venue

Rentals

⭐ **EIGHT TO TEN MONTHS**

When you choose to marry at an off-premise venue, chances are you will be responsible for renting everything. Work with the representatives from the venue and the caterer you hire to find a preferred rental company. These people will be able to provide guidance as to which rentals you will need for that venue and the quantity you will need for your guest count. The representative from the rental company should also work closely with you to construct a rental equipment plan for your wedding.

In addition to basic rental equipment, there are many companies that rent specialty and custom-designed china, flatware, glassware, cakestands, arches, gazebos, gates, aisle decor, coffee tables, couches, and lounge furniture. You name it—you can probably find it. Specialty rentals are not the "necessity" type of rentals you may need for other locations, they are the items that can add that extra pizzazz and enhance your theme or overall design scheme.

Questions to Ask

♥ What is the fee for the rental?

♥ Is there a delivery charge? What are normal delivery hours? When do overtime/extra charges apply?

♥ When can the items be delivered/picked up? Are there additional fees for weekend/off-hour deliveries?

♥ Is a security deposit required? How much? When is it refundable?

♥ Will someone be on site during the event to fix any problems that might arise?

♥ What is the policy for breakage or damage?

Rentals

COMPANY:

CONTACT:

PHONE:

EMAIL:

FAX:

DEPOSIT:

FINAL PAYMENT DUE:

DETAILS:

SPECIAL INSTRUCTIONS:

The Style Makers

5

♥ Floral Design

♥ The Wedding Cake

♥ Lighting

♥ The Wedding Invitations

Once you have decided on the venue, you can begin the fun part of wedding planning: the personal touches that determine and define your style as a couple. These will be reflected in your theme, color scheme, floral design, lighting, linen, your wedding cake, even the stationery and invitations.

Floral Design
★ TEN TO TWELVE MONTHS

Your floral designer's visions are on display to your guests from the moment they arrive at the celebration, and may, therefore, leave the greatest single impression of the style of your wedding in the guests' minds. When selecting your designer, be very sure to interview and hire a professional wedding floral designer—the smaller stores may not be able to handle the workload of a full wedding.

When meeting with a floral designer, take swatches of fabrics, tearsheets from magazines, books, and anything else that will convey your visions, style, and preferences. A professional will welcome your input and work with you to fit those ideas into your wedding and budget. (If you have dislikes or allergies make sure those are known, too!) The floral designer should offer expert advice on seasonal flowers and trends, and should provide you with a detailed proposal outlining floral selections, colors, and pricing.

Questions to Ask
- How many weddings have you designed?
- What is your specialty/style you are known for?
- May we see samples of your work and/or a portfolio of past weddings?
- May we speak with references?
- How many weddings do you handle on one day?
- Do you handle other specialty items such as the aisle runner, pillars, and arches?
- When is the deadline for making changes to my order?
- What is the payment schedule?
- Is there a delivery fee?
- What is the cancellation/postponement policy?

Floral Designer

COMPANY:

CONTACT:

PHONE:

EMAIL:

FAX:

DEPOSIT:

FINAL PAYMENT DUE:

DETAILS:

SPECIAL INSTRUCTIONS:

The Floral Worksheet

You can use the floral worksheet as a checklist to present to the floral designer when you meet to discuss your requirements. Not all sections may apply: simply highlight those you wish to include in your order.

Floral arrangements may leave the greatest impression of your wedding style on guests

Floral Worksheet

- [ ] Personal flowers
- [ ] Bouquets
  - [ ] Bride
  - [ ] Maid/matron of honor
  - [ ] Bridesmaids
  - [ ] Junior bridesmaids
  - [ ] Flower girls
- [ ] Boutonnières
  - [ ] Groom
  - [ ] Best man
  - [ ] Groomsmen
  - [ ] Ushers
  - [ ] Ring/page/train bearers
- [ ] Family
  - [ ] Mother of bride
  - [ ] Mother of groom
  - [ ] Father of the bride
  - [ ] Father of the groom
  - [ ] Siblings
  - [ ] Stepmothers
  - [ ] Stepfathers
  - [ ] Step siblings
  - [ ] Grandmothers
  - [ ] Grandfathers
  - [ ] Special relatives (aunts/uncles, godparents, sponsors, close friends)

- [ ] Miscellaneous
  - [ ] Greeters
  - [ ] Guest book attendant
  - [ ] Readers
  - [ ] Soloists
- [ ] Ceremony venue
  - [ ] Aisle runner
  - [ ] Entrance
  - [ ] Gazebo/arch/chuppah
  - [ ] Guest book table
  - [ ] Pew/aisle decor
  - [ ] Other:
- [ ] Reception venue
  - [ ] Bar
  - [ ] Buffet/food display tables
  - [ ] Cake
  - [ ] Cake knife
  - [ ] Cake table
  - [ ] Cocktail tables
  - [ ] Entrance
  - [ ] Guest book table
  - [ ] Guest tables
  - [ ] Head table/sweetheart table
  - [ ] Place card table
  - [ ] Restrooms
  - [ ] Toasting flutes
  - [ ] Toss bouquet
  - [ ] Other:

The Wedding Cake

⭐ SIX TO EIGHT MONTHS

The wedding cake is the star of the reception and guests eagerly look forward to this part of the proceedings. Cakes are offered in all shapes and sizes—individual cakes, squares, circles, ten-foot tall towers. You name it—there is a pastry chef who can create it (for a price, of course!). You can find referrals for wedding cakes from the venue, your wedding planner, friends, and other vendors. Additionally, there are many venues that offer wedding cakes, either from selected local bakers or from their in-house pastry chef as a part of their package. If the venue offers this option, and you choose not to use it, be aware they may still charge a per-person cake-cutting fee, so remember to confirm this with the venue.

When you meet with a pastry chef, take along your magazine clippings and/or sketches, swatches for the color scheme you have selected, and an approximate guest count.

Questions to Ask

💜 Will you create a custom cake, or must we choose from your "collection"?

💜 What are the options for the flavor, fillings, and frosting?

💜 Are there additional costs for using different flavors of cake and fillings for different tiers of the cake?

💜 How do you price your cakes?

💜 Do you deliver? If so, is that an additional cost?

💜 Will you place fresh flowers on the cake (if required)?

💜 Will you place the topper on the cake?

Wedding Cake Chef

COMPANY:

CONTACT:

PHONE:

EMAIL:

FAX:

DEPOSIT:

FINAL PAYMENT DUE:

DETAILS/DESIGN:

CAKE/FILLING/FROSTING:

Lighting

Event lighting adds warmth, energy, beauty, excitement, and glamor. In conjunction with your florals, linens, and even china selections, the right lighting can transform a venue into a complete environment. Lighting effects can be created simply by washing the walls with color from uplights to more complex designs and images projected on the walls and dance floor. There are many technical challenges involved with event lighting and it is best to leave your lighting needs to a qualified professional event lighting technician.

Questions to Ask

- What type of lighting will best suit our budget and needs for our venue?
- What types of lighting services do you offer?
- May we see a portfolio? May we speak with references?
- Does the venue have adequate power? Will we need a generator?
- Will you accompany me to the site to ensure we have the proper equipment/set up for lighting?
- Does the cost include all of the set up and breakdown and equipment you will need for the event? If not, what is included/excluded?

Lighting Designer

COMPANY:

CONTACT:

PHONE:

EMAIL:

FAX:

DEPOSIT:

FINAL PAYMENT DUE:

DETAILS:

SPECIAL INSTRUCTIONS:

The Wedding Invitations

Selecting Invitations

⭐ **EIGHT TO TEN MONTHS**

You may have already had experience of ordering stationery if you opted for printed engagement announcements. If so, your choice of announcement would have given an indication of the style and formality of the wedding. The invitations themselves should reflect that same style and tone. It is worth looking at the options at an early stage in the planning, especially if you want a highly personalized approach.

There are many styles, types, and pricepoints for wedding invitations. There are numerous resources online, or a fine stationer will be able to show you samples in invitation books. The basic printing styles for invitations, in order of cost and complexity, are:

♥ Custom invitations, which can be created by a graphic artist or sometimes by the bride herself. Due to the time and detail involved, this is typically one of the more expensive options. The basic design process for custom invitations can take many months.

♥ Engraved invitations are the most traditional and formal style of invitations. Engraved invitations have been used for years and have a timeless appeal.

♥ Letterpress invitations are almost the reverse process of engraved invitations. In this instance, the metal plate is actually pressed down into the paper creating a recessed type.

♥ Thermography gives the illusion of engraved invitations without the cost. This is a very cost-effective option, and is one of the most widely used styles of invitation printing.

♥ Offset printing is standard flat printing and can be done from a computer printer or printing machine.

Designing Invitations

 **SIX TO EIGHT MONTHS**

The invitation should complement the overall design and style of your wedding while, of course, conveying the important information to the guests. Traditional invitation books, custom-designed ensembles, do-it-yourself kits from the local craft or stationery stores, and online catalogs provide numerous options for every couple.

Ordering Invitations

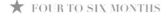 **FOUR TO SIX MONTHS**

When it is time to purchase your invitations, you will need to know the basic facts and details that you would like to include in your invitation. Turnaround times vary with company, design, and printing process.

Having the following information at hand will ease the ordering process and prevent delays in delivery.

♥ Number of invitations you will need. Order extra invitations (say 10–25). It is far less expensive to order a few extra invitations than to place a new order later.

♥ The wording that you would like on the invitations.

♥ Basic ceremony and reception information: dates, times, and addresses.

♥ Will there be an entrée option that you will need to include on the response card?

♥ Give a "respond by" date. If the caterer needs the final guest count one week before the wedding date, you should put a "respond by" date of about two weeks earlier on the response card. This will give you time to follow up with those who have not replied.

Components of an Invitation

A basic invitation ensemble comprises:

- ♥ The wedding invitation and inner and outer envelopes
- ♥ The reception card
- ♥ The response card and envelope
- ♥ Map card or directions

When you order your invitations, you may also wish to include other items of stationery:

- ♥ Wedding announcements
- ♥ Ceremony programs
- ♥ Pew cards
- ♥ Menu cards
- ♥ Escort cards
- ♥ Place cards
- ♥ Thank you cards
- ♥ "At home" cards to announce your new home address

Addressing the Invitations

 THREE MONTHS

Addressing can take between one and four weeks depending on the number of guests, and the speed of the calligrapher. Calligraphy lends a beautiful accent to any wedding invitation. Purists call for the penmanship of a fine calligrapher but modern brides are also opting for computer-generated calligraphy.

ADDRESSING ETIQUETTE There are many options for addressing invitations depending on the invitee. The basics are:

- ♥ The outer envelope is addressed to the invited guests and should include the full names of the guest and the proper titles (Mr. and Mrs. John Henry Smith).
- ♥ The inner envelope should include the title and last names (Mr. and Mrs. Smith).
- ♥ For children under the age of 18, their first names should be listed under the parents' names on the inner envelope, in birth order (oldest to youngest).
- ♥ Children over 18 should receive their own invitation.

Assemble the Invitations

 THREE MONTHS

Begin the assembling and stuffing of the envelopes by developing a system; take the largest component of the ensemble (usually the invitation itself) and stack the remaining items on top in descending size order (largest to smallest). Do not put the response card in the envelope, simply tuck it under the envelope flap. Do not forget the stamp on the response envelope.

Mail the Invitations

 TWO MONTHS

Many invitations require additional postage because of their weight. Currently, many invitations are also requiring additional postage because of their size and shape (oversized and square invitations cost more). Assemble one complete ensemble and take it to the post office to be weighed. When you purchase your postage, be sure to also purchase stamps for the response card as well. The post office offers specialty stamps with love and wedding-related themes.

Invitation Stationer

COMPANY:

CONTACT:

PHONE:

EMAIL:

FAX:

DEPOSIT:

FINAL PAYMENT DUE:

DETAILS:

SPECIAL INSTRUCTIONS:

The Style Makers

The Wedding Party

♥ Select the Wedding Party

♥ Attendants' Responsibilities

♥ Gifts for the Wedding Party

I t often slips the minds of brides and grooms that when they select who is to form their wedding party, it should be about far more than who looks good in a pink strapless dress or a tuxedo—the wedding party has responsibilities. A good wedding party can really help the couple through this crazy and amazing time of their lives and, when all is said and done, each and every member of the party should be thanked appropriately for their part in the celebration.

Select the Wedding Party

★ TEN TO TWELVE MONTHS

The members of the wedding party can include the bride and groom's close friends and family members. The size of the wedding party should reflect the size of the wedding. For instance, a 20-person wedding party with 75 guests would seem out of place. There was a time when the number of bridesmaids and groomsmen had to be even— but that no longer applies.

The wedding party is expected to assist with some wedding planning duties, attend pre-wedding parties, and the rehearsal. Individuals are also expected to pay for their own attire, including shoes and accessories, as well as travel arrangements and accommodation. The bride and groom should provide bouquets or boutonnières, and thank everyone with an appropriate gift, usually given at the rehearsal dinner.

A good wedding party can really help the couple through this crazy and amazing time

Attendants' Responsibilities

Maid/Matron of Honor

- To be the bride's sounding board and confidante
- Generally to assist the bride during her wedding planning and on the day
- To plan and organize the bridal shower and bachelorette party (assisted by the bridesmaids)
- To help shop for the bride's and bridesmaids' dresses
- To coordinate fittings with bridesmaids
- To prepare an emergency kit for the day (assisted by the bridesmaids)
- To act as a liaison with bridesmaids during planning, rehearsal, and on the wedding day
- To help organize attendants at rehearsal and on the wedding day
- To help dress the bride on the wedding day
- To assist with veil and train, including knowing how to bustle train after the ceremony
- To hold bridal bouquet during ceremony
- To witness the signing of the marriage license
- To offer a toast at the reception
- To dance and socialize with guests at the reception
- To ensure (with best man) the bride and groom have a drink and food throughout the day
- To arrange (with the best man) to have a snack and champagne in the couple's hotel room after the ceremony
- To assist (with the best man) with gift collection and delivery to the couple's residence
- To assist the bride with her attire and personal items during transit from ceremony to reception and after

The Best Man

- To be the groom's confidant
- Generally to assist the groom during planning and on the wedding day
- To plan and organize the bachelor party (assisted by the groomsmen)
- To help select/coordinate formalwear with groomsmen
- To act as a liaison with groomsmen during planning, rehearsal, and on the wedding day
- To help dress the groom on the wedding day

- To stand at the altar, immediately beside the groom
- To hold the wedding rings during the ceremony
- To witness the signing of the marriage license
- To assist with the groom's attire and personal items during transit from ceremony to reception and after the ceremony
- To coordinate the return of rented formalwear
- To offer first toast at the reception
- To dance and socialize with guests at the reception
- To ensure (with maid/matron of honor) the bride and groom have a drink and food throughout the day
- To arrange (with maid/matron of honor) to have a snack and champagne in the couple's hotel room after the ceremony
- To assist (with the maid/matron of honor) with gift collection and delivery to the couple's residence
- To pay and/or tip vendors

The Bridesmaids

- To offer general support
- To help plan the bridal shower and/or bachelorette party (under guidance of maid/matron of honor)
- To assist guests at the ceremony and reception
- To help prepare emergency kit (under guidance of maid/matron of honor)
- To assist the bride with pre-wedding tasks (such as address invitations and assemble favors)

The Groomsmen

♥ To offer general support
♥ To help plan the bachelor party (under guidance of best man)
♥ To assist guests at the ceremony and reception
♥ To direct guests to their seats, the restrooms, and other important locations
♥ To dance and socialize with guests at the reception
♥ To perform ushering duties (see below)

Ushers

♥ Groomsmen often act as ushers, but for a large wedding, additional ushers may be necessary. There should be at least one usher for every fifty guests
♥ To greet guests and walk them to their seats prior to processional
♥ To distribute ceremony programs
♥ To hand out written directions to the reception venue after the ceremony or to direct guests to the reception

Roles for Other Important People

There may be younger people who are important members of your entourage. They may include:

♥ Flower girls: aged between four and eight. They immediately precede the bride down the aisle, often dropping flower petals. There may be any number of flower girls.
♥ Ring bearers: also aged between four and eight. They precede the flower girls down the aisle and often carry a ring pillow with "rings" tied on. (Never give a four-year-old the real rings!)
♥ Junior bridesmaids: aged between nine and sixteen. They may precede or follow the bridesmaids (depending on the order of your processional).
♥ Junior groomsmen: aged between nine and sixteen. They may precede or follow the groomsmen (depending on the order of your processional).
♥ Page/train bearers: aged between six and nine years old. They follow the bride down the aisle carrying her train. They may be boys or girls.

Gifts for the Wedding Party

Take the time to select gifts that acknowledge your appreciation of the wedding party's support and assistance. You may choose to buy each attendant a different gift based on their likes, hobbies, and/or personalities or, as many couples do, present the same to all of the bridesmaids, all of the groomsmen, and so on (some suggestions are listed below). You may also want to purchase gifts for your parents and for those who hosted a party for you. Present these gifts at the rehearsal dinner or, for the bridesmaids, at the bridal luncheon.

IDEAS FOR EVERYONE

- Books
- CDs/DVDs
- Concert tickets
- Gift baskets (wine, gourmet food, coffee/tea, entertainment)
- Gift certificates
- Monogrammed attire/accessories

IDEAS FOR LADIES

- Beauty/spa/bath product
- Fashion accessories (purse, wrap, scarf)
- Jewelry
- Perfume
- Spa services

IDEAS FOR MEN

- Collectibles (based on personal interests)
- Cufflinks
- Electronics
- Engraved personal items (pens, money clip, business card holder)
- Sporting equipment
- Tie and handkerchief set

FOR CHILDREN

- Activity totes (filled with projects/toys for the wedding day)
- Educational activities (fun science experiments, beautiful books)
- Toys

FOR YOUR PARENTS

- Album of wedding photos
- Artwork
- Bouquet of flowers (delivered to their home the day after the wedding)
- Champagne or fine wine
- His/her massages or spa day
- Mini vacation (a weekend at their favorite local getaway)

Whatever you choose, the gesture will be appreciated.

7

For the Bride

- ♥ The Wedding Gown
- ♥ Where to Find a Gown
- ♥ Choosing a Gown
- ♥ Accessories
- ♥ Personal Grooming
- ♥ Wedding-day Beauty

It is all about the beautiful bride, right? All eyes will be on you—including the camera lenses. This chapter covers everything you need to know and think about—from gown, veil, and shoes, to lingerie, hairstyle, and waxing—to make yourself the most gorgeous, confident, and proud you have ever looked and felt for the great day. You'll want to look at the photographs and films for years to come and re-live the pleasures time and time again.

The Wedding Gown

★ EIGHT TO TEN MONTHS

Your wedding gown may be the most expensive and exquisite garment you will ever own. With contemporary gown designers providing almost limitless options in silhouettes, colors, fabrics, and price ranges, the search for "the dress" can seem very daunting. Yet, by approaching gown shopping logically, the experience can be memorable for all the right reasons.

Begin your gown search by exploring your options (see "Where to Find a Gown" opposite). Start shopping early, as it takes four to six months to receive a gown after placing the order. Be sure to allow plenty of time for your search so that you avoid rush charges on the final order. These charges average 10–20 percent of the cost of the dress, and are a needless expense.

Your gown may be the most exquisite garment you will ever own

Bridal Salon

COMPANY:

CONTACT:

PHONE:

EMAIL:

FAX:

DEPOSIT:

FINAL PAYMENT:

DELIVERY DATE:

SPECIAL INSTRUCTIONS:

DETAILS:

Where to Find a Gown

When it comes to finding the gown of your dreams, you have many options.

The Bridal Salon

Salons offer personal attention and a full range of services for the bride. They carry a wide selection of gown styles, veils, and accessories to complete the total bridal look. Many offer alterations on site. When you arrive for your appointment, try to be early so that you can browse through the various gowns and accessories. A fun perk of shopping at a salon are designer "trunk shows"—special in-store events that give you the opportunity to preview the newest selection of designs, possibly meet the designer, and sometimes receive a promotional price on that designer's gown on that day.

Heirloom Dress or Couture Creation

These are more unique options for gown selection. If you choose to wear a family heirloom or a historical/vintage gown, be sure to find a couturiere who is skilled in restoring and working with heirloom dresses. If you have always envisioned your wedding gown, the custom route may be for you. Working with a professional, you can design and create the gown of your dreams using the fabrics you select. Your gown will be unique, and it will be made to fit you perfectly.

Other Options

It is becoming more popular to go gown shopping on the web, off the rack, and through rental stores. Bridal discounters/consignment/Internet auction sites provide a highly cost-effective solution if you are budget-conscious. You can find a range of styles, from the "not so new," to designer knock offs, or brides selling designer gowns for a fraction of the original cost. If you prefer a less formal gown or are on a tight timeframe, try a department store or designer boutique. You can inspect, try on, and purchase the dress then and there. Finally, some brides choose the rental route, wearing a designer gown for a fraction of the cost of purchasing a designer gown.

Choosing a Gown

Once you have decided where to shop for your gown, review these points:

- Do your research. Rule out what you don't want if you can't decide what you do want.
- Set a budget for the entire bridal ensemble. This includes alterations, undergarments, a veil and/or headpiece, shoes, jewelry, and possibly a crinoline/slip.
- Think about color. Do you want a white dress? Is ivory or another color an option? What about an accent color or a touch of color?
- What style of wedding are you planning: formal, semi-formal, or casual? What will the season be? The time of day? Will there be a theme?
- Where are you intending to hold the ceremony/reception? Will you marry in a house of worship? Will the location be outdoors or indoors?
- Are there cultural or religious considerations to take into account?
- What do you feel comfortable wearing? Think about your regular wardrobe; decide what flatters you. Also, know your own figure—the gown should accentuate the positives and camouflage the negatives.

When it is time to head to the salon/store/seamstress, try the following:

- Make an appointment and be on time.
- Take only one or two people with you.
- State your budget.
- Take any accessories you definitely plan to wear to make sure they work with your gown.
- Wear appropriate lingerie and shoes (heel height).
- Take photos of dresses that you like and show them to the consultant. Keep an open mind when trying the gowns. Sales consultants know their inventory and may be privy to gowns that would be great for you, but are not widely advertised.
- When it is time to purchase a gown, be sure to thoroughly read and understand your contract/receipt.
- If you intend to look at veils and headpieces, take photos of the hairstyle you plan (up/down/curly/straight) or wear your hair in that style.

Choosing a Silhouette

There are four basic types of silhouette to choose from. Your choice should be governed by what feels most comfortable, and what is the most appropriate silhouette for the shape of your body.

- Ball gown: the most traditional look, it features a full skirt and a fitted bodice. It is suitable for most figures, but best avoided if you are quite short or petite.
- Empire: a neoclassical look, it features a very high waist that accentuates the bust and helps conceal the waist and hips.
- Princess: also known as the "A-line". This style is a popular choice for most body shapes, but is not suitable if you are thick-waisted.
- Sheath: a close-fitting style that is most suited for tall, thin women or those with petite figures.

Fitting the Gown

Once the gown comes in, you will be able to begin the fitting process. The gown will come in based on how your measurements fall into the designer's size chart. Be prepared for your gown to be altered by the store's seamstress to fit your figure. Most salons offer this service, as do a selection of dressmakers. Be sure to get referrals and entrust your dress only to someone with a spectacular reputation. You may need between one and three fittings, depending on the extent of alterations and any weight fluctuations. It is very important to wear your wedding-day lingerie when being fitted and your wedding-day shoes when it is time to finalize the hem.

You know your own figure— think about what flatters you and accentuates your positives

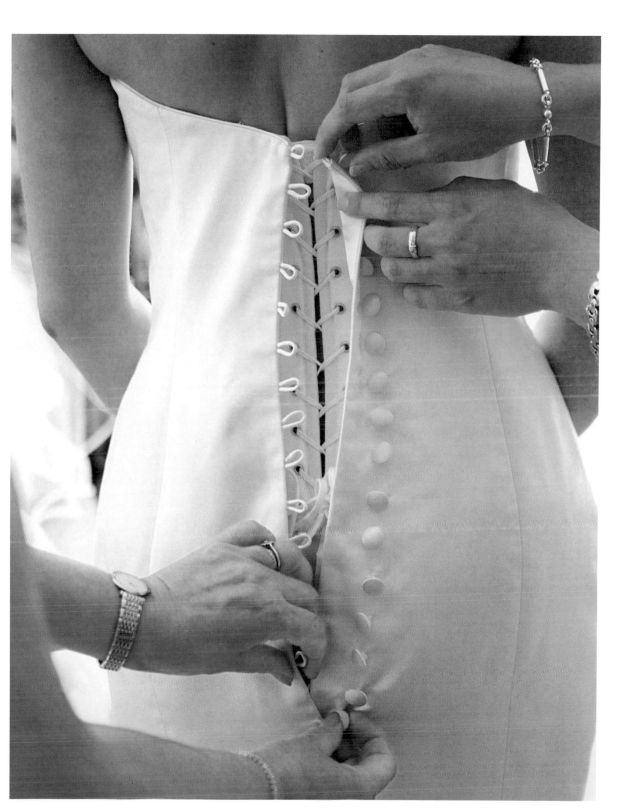

Accessories

To complete your bridal ensemble you will need a range of accessories. Full service bridal salons, department stores, and specialty stores carry an assortment of the following to assist you in creating a total bridal look:

♥ Lingerie: This can include a bustier, corset, crinoline, and nylons. These create the foundation of your bridal look—the wrong choice can ruin the look of the gown.

♥ Veil/Headpiece: The veil/headpiece should complement your gown. Prior to purchasing, you may want to consult with a hair stylist to ensure the veil/headpiece and hairstyle you envision will work together.

♥ Shoes: Many brides select two pairs of shoes; one for the ceremony and a more casual, comfortable pair for the reception. You will need to have your shoes purchased prior to your fittings so that the gown can be properly hemmed.

♥ Purse: A cute purse or small bag for your lipstick and a few essentials is always a good choice.

♥ Jewelry: Jewelry is the final perfecting detail. Keep the jewelry selections in line with the style of the gown. If you have a piece of jewelry you know you will be wearing, take it with you when you go gown shopping.

♥ Second Gown: It is a new trend to have a second dress on hand for the reception. In some cultures, it is customary to change gowns throughout the day and evening. You may choose to do this for comfort or to honor your heritage.

♥ Other Items: Consider gloves if they will complement your dress. A wrap, especially for an evening wedding, is a chic addition to the reception look.

Personal Grooming

★ TEN MONTHS

Your wedding day is one of the most important moments in your life; it makes sense that you want to look the part. Whether that means keeping up with your tried-and-true beauty regime or beginning a new one, now is the time to start preparing.

Review the following list—some of the items may already be part of your regular beauty regime. Determine which additional steps you may wish to take to ensure complete bridal beauty.

- Drink plenty of water to hydrate your skin and keep you healthy.
- Begin an exercise routine; even just taking long walks is beneficial.
- Eat properly.
- Consult with an esthetician and begin a skincare program that includes regular facials and possibly other specialty treatments.
- Continue with your regular hair stylist for cut and color upkeep.
- Consider having your teeth professionally whitened or try over-the-counter products.
- Pamper yourself with a massage now and then.
- Have your eyebrows designed by a professional and maintain the design with regular waxing.
- Have regular manicures and pedicures.

On your wedding day you will naturally want to be at your most beautiful

Wedding-day Beauty

★ SIX TO EIGHT MONTHS

On your wedding day you want to be at your most beautiful. It is worth hiring a professional hair and makeup artist who will come to your home or hotel room on the wedding day, rather than you having to travel to them. Many companies offer these services for very reasonable rates.

Stylists book up quickly during popular wedding months, so do not leave this detail until the last minute. Ask for referrals and always make sure the stylist offers a pre-wedding day session one to two months prior to the wedding so that you can preview your wedding-day look and make any necessary changes. If you do not already have your veil/headpiece selected by this time, take photos or ideas with you to assist the stylist in creating your look.

Questions to Ask

💜 Can you accommodate a group (the bridesmaids) or just the bride on the wedding day?

💜 Will you travel to the hotel or wedding site for these services?

💜 How much do the services cost?

💜 Will you meet with me to discuss veil/headpiece options to suit my hairstyle?

💜 Do you offer a pre-wedding preview for the bride? Is it included in the cost? If not, how much is it?

💜 How much time do you need (in total or per person) on the wedding day?

💜 Are there any special preparations that need to be made in advance (how much space, how many electrical outlets)?

💜 Do we need to bring any of our own cosmetics or hair products?

Hair Stylist

COMPANY:

CONTACT:

PHONE:

EMAIL:

FAX:

DEPOSIT:

FINAL PAYMENT:

SPECIAL INSTRUCTIONS:

DETAILS:

Makeup Stylist

COMPANY:

CONTACT:

PHONE:

EMAIL:

FAX:

DEPOSIT:

FINAL PAYMENT:

SPECIAL INSTRUCTIONS:

DETAILS:

Outfitting the Entourage

8

- ♥ Dressing the Groom
- ♥ Dressing the Wedding Party
- ♥ Tips for Dressing Everyone

As far as attire, hairstyle, grooming, and makeup goes, weddings are still mainly about the bride, but it is the groom's big day too, and your intended has a number of choices over how he is turned out—as do the bridal entourage and the family members. Keeping everyone in the wedding party looking terrific is also important! Good communication pays, so that no one wears clashing colors or, as can happen, buys an identical outfit.

Dressing the Groom

Often a groom's workwear will influence his wedding attire. A man who wears a business suit each day may feel he must wear a tuxedo (or even tails) to his wedding in order to be more formal than his daily life. The groom will also need to select a style of shirt, preferred collar, neckwear, and accessories such as cufflinks, button covers, vest, tie, and/or pocket squares to complete the look. Tuxedo or tails are the classic options for grooms, though many men choose attire that reflects their heritage.

The groom should visit a formalwear store, clothing store, or costume shop (depending on his selection of attire) with either the bride or his best man and try on various styles. The wedding venue and the bride's final decision on a gown should highly influence the groom's choice. Bride and groom need to work together, making sure his attire will complement hers. Once he makes his decision, he should look for variations on the style for his groomsmen, the fathers, ushers, and ring bearers.

Personal Grooming

It is not only the bride who is there to wow. Many grooms are taking this to heart and establishing their own "beauty routine." For example:

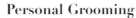

- Drink plenty of water.
- Begin an exercise routine.
- Eat properly and consume alcohol in moderation.
- For problem skin, consult with an esthetician and institute a skincare program.
- Continue with your regular hair stylist for cut and color upkeep.
- Consider having your teeth professionally whitened or try over-the-counter products.
- Pamper yourself with a luxurious massage.
- Have your eyebrows designed by a professional and maintain the design with regular waxing.
- Get a manicure.

Dressing the Wedding Party

Dressing the Bride's Attendants

There are many options for outfitting the women of the wedding party. Dress manufacturers are creating stylish, fashion-forward looks, as well as designing separates and mix-and-match ensembles that are the ideal solutions to this wedding dressing dilemma. With these options available, the bride can dress everyone in the same color and fabric, and select necklines, sleeve lengths, and silhouettes that flatter each individual woman.

Most brides still tend to look for bridesmaids' dresses at traditional salons and shops catering to the bridal industry. However, keeping an open mind and looking for "off-the-rack" (ready-to-wear) dresses at department and specialty stores saves you both time and money. Hiring a professional dressmaker is also an option for dressing the ladies. If you are Internet wise you may be able to find some great deals online.

Begin looking for bridesmaids' dresses six to eight months prior to the wedding. When you order, expect there to be alterations needed, and make sure you allot enough time for that. Collect the measurements of the bridesmaids or have them professionally measured at the salon or by a local dressmaker in their town. When the women attend their final fittings, remind them to take/wear proper undergarments and shoes. To complement the bridesmaids' attire, you may wish to select and have them purchase a combination of the following accessories: earrings, necklaces, bracelets, hair clips and pins, wraps, nylons, purses, and shoes.

Look for dresses at department stores and online to save you both time and money

**DRESSING A MALE ATTENDANT ON THE
BRIDE'S SIDE** The most logical option for a bridesman
or man of honor is to wear a tuxedo, a suit, or other attire
similar to what the groomsmen will wear. He can be
distinguished with a different, but coordinating, vest and
accessories. He usually wears a boutonnière.

**DRESSING THE JUNIOR BRIDESMAIDS, FLOWER
GIRLS/TRAIN BEARERS** Junior bridesmaids often
wear a look that is similar in color and style to the
bridesmaids'. If the bridesmaids' dresses have a very
grown-up look, the junior bridesmaids' version should be
similar, but age-appropriate. They typically carry a bouquet
of flowers, slightly smaller than the bridesmaids'.

White or ivory, depending on the color of your dress, are
popular color options for the flower girls and train
bearers. You can add a dash of color to their attire with
flowers, ribbons, or sashes. Their look is often completed
with a head wreath or headband of flowers, and a purse or
basket of flower petals.

Dressing the Mothers

The mothers must no longer settle for matronly
ensembles! Chic boutiques and high-end department
stores offer tremendous options and designer looks for
both the mother of the bride and the mother of the
groom. The most important factor when selecting the
mothers' attire is to keep with the overall style and theme
of the wedding. If the bridesmaids are wearing taupe,
the mothers should not show up in turquoise blue.
It is traditional for the mother of the groom to allow
the mother of the bride to select her attire first and then
select a complementary color/look (they do not need to
match, just complement each other).

*Add a dash of color to
bridesmaids' outfits with
flowers, ribbons, or sashes*

The Bridesmaids

COMPANY:

CONTACT:

PHONE:

EMAIL:

FAX:

DEPOSIT/DATE ORDERED:

FINAL PAYMENT/DELIVERY DATE:

SPECIAL INSTRUCTIONS:

DRESS DETAILS:

STYLE NUMBER:

COLOR:

DESCRIPTION:

SHOES:

OTHER ACCESSORIES:

	NAME	PHONE	HEIGHT	SIZE	SHOE
MAID/MATRON OF HONOR:					
BRIDESMAID 1:					
BRIDESMAID 2:					
BRIDESMAID 3:					
BRIDESMAID 4:					
BRIDESMAID 5:					
BRIDESMAID 6:					
JUNIOR BRIDESMAID:					
JUNIOR BRIDESMAID:					
FLOWER GIRL:					
FLOWER GIRL:					
FLOWER GIRL:					

The Mothers

THE BRIDE'S MOTHER

DRESS DETAILS:

STYLE NUMBER:

COLOR:

DESCRIPTION:

SHOES:

OTHER ACCESSORIES:

THE GROOM'S MOTHER

DRESS DETAILS:

STYLE NUMBER:

COLOR:

DESCRIPTION:

SHOES:

OTHER ACCESSORIES:

Dressing the Groom's Attendants

The groom's attire will dictate what his attendants wear. If the groom chooses a formal suit or tuxedo, the men typically dress the same. If the groom goes for the non-traditional look, more often than not the men will, too.

When accessorizing a suit or tuxedo, the choices tend to be simple. Color and personalization are achieved in the selection of ties/bow ties and vests. Cufflinks, button covers, or pocket squares (if using) complete the look.

Tuxedos and most suits can be rented from formalwear retailers, men's clothing stores, and even bridal salons. Less traditional attire may be purchased at department or specialty stores or rented from costume shops. Tuxedos can be ordered only a couple of months prior to the wedding date, but if possible, take care of this detail early, as you are counting on many people to get measured and place their orders. The best man should assist the groom in collecting measurements and/or getting the men into a formalwear shop in their area to be measured.

DRESSING A FEMALE ATTENDANT ON THE GROOM'S SIDE Options for a groomswoman or best woman include a tuxedo tailored to fit a woman, skirted tuxedo ensembles, a black dress (less elaborate than the bridesmaids or bride) or a dress to match the bridesmaids. These ladies can carry a bouquet or wear a boutonnière.

DRESSING THE USHERS Ushers/escorts have a choice of different looks depending on the formality of the wedding and their duties. They may wear their own dark suit, but generally they will wear something similar in style to the groomsmen with slightly different accessories. Themed attire is also an option.

DRESSING THE JUNIOR GROOMSMEN See "Dressing the Groom's Attendants" opposite.

DRESSING THE RING BEARER/PAGES Ring bearers and pages usually wear pint-sized tuxedos that can be rented from formalwear shops, but they can wear themed attire. The ring bearer usually carries a decorative pillow down the aisle. Pillows can be purchased at bridal salons, stationery stores, party supply stores, and online.

Dressing the Fathers

Both the father of the bride and the father of the groom often wear tuxedos, formal suits, or themed attire to coordinate with the wedding party and to set themselves apart from the guests. Different color accessories can be worn to distinguish them from the groomsmen

Tips for Dressing Everyone

With so many people to manage, dress, and accessorize, it is good to have some quick-reference tips:

💜 Before you begin dressing the wedding party, it is important to have your own dress selected and know what style of suit or tuxedo the groom will be wearing; your choice of attire should be reflected in the clothes of the wedding party, not upstaged by it.

💜 Rather than have your bridesmaids buy matching shoes, let them wear shoes of their own selection in a complementary color to the dress. They will love you for not making them purchase (often uncomfortable) dyed-to-match shoes. Be sure to give them guidelines and pick the shade or color.

💜 Let the men do the same and wear their own dress shoes. Rented shoes can be uncomfortable.

💜 You can let the men wear pocket squares instead of boutonnières. A pocket square and a boutonnière are traditionally not worn at the same time.

💜 Ask the men to unpack rented ensembles and to double check they have everything they need: suspenders, vest, tie, shirt, pants, jacket, button covers, and cufflinks. Remind them to wear black socks and a white undershirt on the wedding day.

💜 Many mothers do not want a floral corsage pinned to their very expensive ensemble. Wrist corsages are a great alternative, as are small floral bouquets A few flowers tied together with a pretty ribbon are convenient for the mothers to carry during the ceremony and photo sessions, and are easily laid down on the table during the reception.

The Men

COMPANY:

CONTACT:

PHONE:

EMAIL:

FAX:

DEPOSIT/DATE ORDERED:

FINAL PAYMENT/DELIVERY DATE:

SPECIAL INSTRUCTIONS:

GROOM

HEIGHT:

SUIT SIZE:

SHOE SIZE:

TUXEDO STYLE:

COLOR:

SHOES:

ACCESSORIES:

DATE ORDERED:

PICKUP DATE:

THE GROOMSMEN

TUXEDO STYLE:

COLOR:

SHOES:

ACCESSORIES:

DATE ORDERED:

PICKUP DATE:

	NAME	PHONE	HEIGHT	SIZE	SHOE
BEST MAN:					
GROOMSMAN 1:					
GROOMSMAN 2:					
GROOMSMAN 3:					
GROOMSMAN 4:					
GROOMSMAN 5:					
GROOMSMAN 6:					
JUNIOR GROOMSMAN:					
JUNIOR GROOMSMAN:					
PAGE/TRAIN BEARER:					
PAGE/TRAIN BEARER:					
RING BEARER:					
USHER:					
USHER:					
USHER:					
USHER:					

BRIDE'S FATHER

STYLE NUMBER:

COLOR:

SHOES:

DATE ORDERED:

PICKUP DATE:

GROOM'S FATHER

STYLE NUMBER:

COLOR:

SHOES:

DATE ORDERED:

PICKUP DATE:

9 Parties

- ♥ Bridal Shower
- ♥ Bridal Luncheon
- ♥ Bachelor & Bachelorette Parties
- ♥ The Rehearsal Dinner
- ♥ Other Parties

Planning a wedding is not only about the ceremony and the reception. It is also about celebrations before and after the wedding day. Couples have found numerous ways to extend their wedding festivities—bridal showers are turning into spa days, bachelor and bachelorette parties become long weekends on the beach, and pre-wedding activities and post-wedding brunches are almost a necessity.

Bridal Shower

★ ATTEND TWO TO FOUR MONTHS

The bridal shower is an opportunity to share the pre-wedding experience with friends and family and to get some great gifts for your new home and/or honeymoon. It is usually held between a couple of months and a couple of weeks prior to the wedding, and the maid/matron of honor, assisted by the bridesmaids, often acts as hostess.

Depending on the size of the wedding, your number of friends, and the size of your family, you may want to convert one large shower into several smaller showers. More intimate showers give the guests a chance to spend time with you, as well as giving more people the opportunity to host. For example, your bridesmaids can host the "friend" shower; an aunt, the "family" shower; and co-workers could organize something during a lunch hour. And do not forget the couples' shower, including the groom and all friends.

The people invited to the shower(s) should include only invited wedding guests. If you are having multiple showers, the bridesmaids and mothers are typically invited to all the showers, however, they do not and should not be expected to bring a gift to each one.

Bridal Showers

SHOWER #1

DATE:

TIME:

HOSTESS:

LOCATION:

THEME:

SHOWER #2

DATE:

TIME:

HOSTESS:

LOCATION:

THEME:

Bridal Luncheon

★ PLAN SIX TO EIGHT MONTHS HOST ONE DAY TO ONE WEEK

The bridal luncheon is a long-standing tradition. It is hosted by the bride, normally a couple of days prior to the wedding day, once all the bridesmaids have gathered in town for the festivities. This luncheon is not a requirement, but it is a great opportunity for some special "girl time" before the wedding. Many brides have added their own spin to the bridal luncheon, offering the bridesmaids a chance to have manicures, pedicures, and massages prior to the wedding. The bride may present the bridesmaids' gifts at this time. Often the mothers are invited as well.

Bridal Luncheon

DATE:

TIME:

LOCATION:

CONTACT PERSON:

PHONE NUMBER:

EMAIL:

ADDRESS:

DEPOSIT DUE/DEPOSIT PAID:

FINAL GUEST COUNT DUE:

NOTES:

Bachelor & Bachelorette Parties

★ ATTEND ONE TO FOUR WEEKS

The first thoughts that often come to mind when you hear mention of a bachelor or bachelorette party may be shots of tequila and strippers, but there are also more refined versions too. Organized by the best man and maid/matron of honor respectively, these parties have evolved to include spa days, sporting events, dinner and clubbing as great alternatives to the "traditional" raucous bachelor or bachelorette party. You need not restrict yourself to just going out for one evening: another popular option is the bachelor/bachelorette weekend. Imagine an entire weekend celebrating the end of your single days!

Hosting the Fun

Bachelor and bachelorette parties are held within a couple of weeks or days before the wedding, and include your closest friends—usually the adult members of your wedding party. The host/hostess(es) may pay for the party or meet part of the cost, but more often than not, everyone is responsible for paying for his- or herself, and also contributes to a group fund to pay for the groom/bride.

Imagine an entire weekend celebrating the end of your single days

Party Plans

BACHELORETTE PARTY

DATE:

TIME:

LOCATION:

THEME:

ORGANIZED BY:

BACHELOR PARTY

DATE:

TIME:

LOCATION:

THEME:

ORGANIZED BY:

The Rehearsal Dinner

★ PLAN SIX TO EIGHT MONTHS/ATTEND ONE TO TWO DAYS

The rehearsal dinner is traditionally hosted by the groom's family and is an intimate celebration with the two families and your wedding party. This dinner, held immediately following the ceremony rehearsal (see page 133), is an opportunity for everyone to socialize or get to know one another better, and should not be more formal than the wedding. It is a great time for saying thank you to important people, and is often the occasion when the bride and groom will present their attendants and parents with gifts. Also it is a great opportunity to make more personal speeches and toasts.

The guest list for the dinner should include your parents and other immediate family, the Ceremony Officiant and his/her spouse, members of your wedding party and their spouses/steady significant others, and the parents of any small children in the wedding party (if the children will be invited to the dinner, as usually the hour is late for small children). Many couples will also want to include extended family and out-of-town guests, making for quite a large dinner. It is really up to you, your fiancé, and his parents (assuming they are the hosts) to create a reasonable guest list. This, like other matters involving invitees and money, may cause stress. Instead, you may choose to have a very intimate party with only the wedding party and parents.

The rehearsal dinner is a great time for saying thank you to important people

Rehearsal Dinner

DATE:

TIME:

LOCATION AND ADDRESS:

CONTACT:

PHONE:

EMAIL:

HOSTS OF DINNER:

NUMBER OF GUESTS:

TIME CONSTRAINTS:

ATTIRE:

TOASTS AND ANNOUNCEMENTS:

DECORATIONS:

MENU:

AGENDA FOR THE EVENING:

Parties

Other Parties

★ PLAN SIX TO EIGHT MONTHS
ATTEND ONE DAY PRIOR, ONE DAY AFTER

Welcome Party

If many guests are traveling from out of town, it is a
courteous gesture to organize a gathering for them.
A welcome party can be anything from an elaborate feast
to a barbecue in the backyard, and is usually held a night
or two before the wedding. Be careful and clever if the
budget is an issue for you—consider a gathering at a close
friend's or relative's home, or maybe just a cocktail
reception at the guests' hotel. Invitations should be
extended to the guests in your save-the-date cards and
in the welcome letter left for the guests at their hotel.

Welcome Party

DATE:
....

TIME:
....

LOCATION AND ADDRESS:
....

CONTACT:
....

PHONE:
....

EMAIL:
....

HOST:
....

NUMBER OF GUESTS:
....

TIME CONSTRAINTS:
....

THEME/DECOR:
....
....

MENU:
....
....

AGENDA FOR THE EVENING:

Post-Wedding Brunch

The post-wedding brunch is typically held at a central location, either a local hotel or restaurant, or even the family home on the morning following the wedding. You and your new husband do not have an obligation to attend, but it can be a great finale for the wedding festivities and an opportunity to show your appreciation to the guests for attending the wedding. The brunch is usually attended by out-of-town guests, but should be offered to all wedding guests. If the brunch is held at the parent's home, it presents an opportunity for gifts to be opened. Again, invitations should be extended to the guests in your save-the-date cards and in the welcome letter left for the guests at their hotel.

Post-Wedding Brunch

DATE:

TIME:

LOCATION AND ADDRESS:

CONTACT:

PHONE:

EMAIL:

HOST:

NUMBER OF GUESTS:

TIME CONSTRAINTS:

THEME/DECOR:

MENU:

AGENDA:

10

The Guests

- ♥ Save-the-Date Cards
- ♥ Accommodation
- ♥ Transportation
- ♥ Wedding Favors
- ♥ Welcome Gifts

D o not forget that you and your fiancé are the hosts of this event. As such, you should attend to every arrangement to make this experience wonderful for your guests. Start with giving timely information about the wedding date and time, accommodation, and transportation. To show your appreciation to your guests, they should be welcomed upon their arrival at the hotel, thanked with favors at the reception, and, if possible, included in the pre- and post-wedding festivities.

Save-the-Date Cards

★ ORDER EIGHT TO TEN MONTHS/MAIL SIX TO EIGHT MONTHS

Save-the-date cards are a great way to notify friends and family of the date of your wedding. These cards are not necessary but thoughtful, especially if you have many guests attending from out of town. Save-the-date cards should be sent between six and eight months prior to the wedding date—enough time for guests to begin making necessary arrangements in their schedules but not too late as to compete with the sending of the actual wedding invitation. Only send a save-the-date card to those people you are positive will be invited.

Wording the Cards

The cards may be fairly simple and state the basic facts, or they may be more elaborate, giving guests a taste of the magnitude of the events that await, as well as supplying the necessary information. The information on save-the-date cards must always include:

♥ Names of the bride and groom
♥ Date of the wedding
♥ Location (city and state) of the wedding
♥ Host of wedding (if not bride and groom)

In addition, you should also provide the following practical information (this typically does not get printed on the actual save-the-date card but on another card or separate paper):

♥ Information and rates for lodging/accommodation
♥ Transportation information (rental car, taxi, buses, town car/limousines, luxury coaches)
♥ Travel information (how to get there by plane, train, or automobile)
♥ Relevant local information (climate, weather, traffic)
♥ Local places of interest guests may wish to visit
♥ Pre-/post-wedding parties (welcome party, rehearsal dinner, post-wedding brunch)

Accommodation

★ EIGHT TO TEN MONTHS

It is thoughtful to arrange accommodation at local hotels for out-of-town guests. Call a few hotels (in different price ranges) in the area and set up room blocks for your guests. Hotels often offer a discounted rate for groups. The special rates will be available for a specified period of time (deadline is usually one or two months prior to the wedding date). Inform guests of any offers through email, your wedding website, or on the save-the-date card.

While you are researching accommodation for your guests, take a moment to think about where you will stay the night before the wedding, where you (and the entourage) will get ready on the wedding day, and where you will spend your first night as a married couple. Ask about possible deals on rooms at the hotel where your guests are staying or where you are holding the reception.

Accommodation Arrangements

GUEST LODGING	ACCOMMODATION FOR YOUR WEDDING NIGHT
LOCATION:	LOCATION:
CONTACT:	CONTACT:
PHONE:	PHONE:
EMAIL:	EMAIL:
ADDRESS:	ADDRESS:
RATE:	RATE:
CUTOFF DATE FOR SPECIAL RATE:	NOTES:
GROUP NUMBER/GROUP NAME:	
TYPE OF ROOM:	
SHUTTLE SERVICE TO AND FROM AIRPORT: YES/NO	

Transportation

★ EIGHT TO TEN MONTHS

Wherever guests are traveling from, it is courteous to arrange for wedding day transportation. Providing luxury coaches or shuttles not only alleviates the stress of navigating, but allows everyone to enjoy the festivities without mixing alcohol and driving. Include information about pick-up times and locations with your save-the-date cards, wedding website, and/or welcome letter.

Most guests will be in town for several days. It would be thoughtful, therefore, to provide your guests with the names of companies that provide rental cars, taxis, town cars, or limousines in the area. Depending on your city, information on public transportation may also be helpful. Again, include this information in your save-the-date cards, wedding website, and/or welcome letter.

Transportation Arrangements

LUXURY COACHES/SHUTTLES	LIMOUSINE/TOWN CAR
COMPANY:	COMPANY:
CONTACT:	CONTACT:
PHONE:	PHONE:
EMAIL:	EMAIL:
FAX:	FAX:
DEPOSIT:	DEPOSIT:
FINAL PAYMENT:	FINAL PAYMENT:
SPECIAL INSTRUCTIONS:	SPECIAL INSTRUCTIONS:
DETAILS:	DETAILS:
TAXI SERVICE	RENTAL CARS
COMPANY:	COMPANY:
CONTACT:	CONTACT:
PHONE:	PHONE:
EMAIL:	EMAIL:
FAX:	FAX:
DETAILS:	DETAILS:

Wedding Favors

⭐ SIX TO EIGHT MONTHS

Wedding favors are a small gift that you and your husband present to guests as a way of thanking everyone for being part of the event. They are a traditional component of a wedding celebration, typically placed at the guest's place setting at the reception, but in choosing what to give you can be quite personal and creative. There are numerous websites that specialize in selling wedding favors such as bells and picture frames. The overall style or theme of your wedding, your special interests or favorite edibles also make great favors. Here are some further ideas:

- ♥ Specialty chocolates, cookies, or other treats
- ♥ Gourmet treat from the region in which you are marrying
- ♥ CD containing your favorite songs
- ♥ Splits of wine or champagne
- ♥ Wedding tea or coffee
- ♥ Donation to a favorite charity (in lieu of each guest receiving a gift)

Ideas for Favors

ITEM	COST (PER FAVOR)

Welcome Gifts

⭐ FOUR TO SIX MONTHS

After a long journey, how welcoming to walk into your hotel room and discover a thoughtful treat. While it is not a necessity, it is certainly a nice touch to receive a welcome gift from the bride and groom, and guests often expect a little something. You can prepare your welcome gift yourself, enlist help from the wedding party, purchase prepared gift baskets, or hire a company to prepare specialized gifts. You will need to know the number of guests and who is staying where to arrange for gifts to be delivered. Call the hotels where you have arranged room blocks and ask for a list of guests and when they are checking in. You may need to call some of the out-of-towners for confirmation of their arrangements.

Your welcome gift need not be elaborate. It might be bottled waters, snacks, a deck of playing cards, activity kits for travelers with children, wine (don't forget a corkscrew!), freshly baked cookies, bath products, or any combination of these. Welcome gifts should always include a welcome letter, a personal note thanking your guests for coming, and provide information on wedding activities. It is an idea to recap information on, for example, transport arrangements (include taxi cab numbers again, just in case), the welcome party, rehearsal dinner, and post-wedding brunch. It is also a good idea to give your guests a map and information on the local area and attractions which you can get from a visitors' bureau.

Wedding Vendors

11

- ♥ Selecting Wedding Vendors
- ♥ Photography
- ♥ Videography/Cinematography

Wedding vendors can truly make or break the day. Finding professional and reputable vendors to provide service on the wedding day is of the utmost importance. When all is said and done, beyond the fond memories, all that is left after the wedding are the photographs, the video, and the guests' well wishes. This chapter includes tips and advice for ensuring your vendors don't let you down.

Selecting Wedding Vendors
★ THROUGHOUT PLANNING

A recurring theme in your wedding planning is hiring the wedding vendors. As you look into vendors, it is quickly apparent that there is really no shortage of professionals in any given category. Because of this, you must do your research and call references. Finding the professionals who offer the right combination of product, price, and personality takes time, but it is time well spent.

Getting Started
Knowing where to look and what to look for will narrow down the choices. You might start with bridal shows, referral lists from your ceremony/reception venues, the Internet, local/regional bridal magazines, wedding resource/planning showrooms, and wedding planners. One of the best anecdotal sources are other brides, and recently married friends and family. These people will give you honest, no-nonsense answers and opinions.

Once you have completed your research, rank your top three to five selections in each category and call each vendor in turn. From the first phone call you can gauge a vendor's professionalism and personality. Asking them some basic questions (see below) should give you an indication of whether or not you would like to meet with that vendor. If a vendor is rude, derogatory, or condescending on the phone when trying to get your business, the service probably won't get any better if you book them (and they have your money).

Questions to Ask
♥ Are you available on my wedding day?
♥ Are you the person I will be working with? If not, may I meet with the person who will be there on my wedding day? (This situation can arise if a photography studio has many photographers who cover weddings.)
♥ What is the average price range for your services? (It will be easier for some vendors to quote this in an initial conversation so that if the prices of the vendor's services are beyond your budget, you know not to continue the process.)
♥ How would you describe your style? (Not relevant to all vendors.)

If you are satisfied with the vendor's answers and they are available on your wedding day, schedule a meeting. This is an essential meeting where you will be assessing the vendor's work, professionalism, presentation, and overall demeanor. Plan to meet face-to-face with at least three vendors in each category, unless you are already familiar with a vendor's work (for example, if your sister used the same florist or a close friend used the wedding planner). Remember you are the client and the vendor should be trying to impress you and assure you of a good service.

Deciding on a Vendor

After these vendor interviews, evaluate each one and rank them on a scale of one to ten. Then ask yourself the following before making your decision:

- ♥ Is the vendor someone I feel I can work with over several months (or even a year)?
- ♥ Does the vendor offer an affordable package/pricing?
- ♥ How does the vendor compare with others in the same category (for example, the price or package)?
- ♥ Is he/she willing and able to accommodate my special requests?
- ♥ Has he/she been responsive to my questions and inquiries?
- ♥ Does he/she act professionally?
- ♥ Did he/she have current professional material/referral letters/samples of his/her work for me to review?

Once you have made a decision, you must get a written contract. Call the vendor right away (the best book up quickly!) to confirm the details and request a contract. The contract should outline specifics such as dates, times, name/names of providers, and types of services/products provided. It will also spell out payment plans, refund and cancellation policies. Do not assume you have secured a vendor for your wedding day until you have a copy of a contract that is signed by you and the vendor. Be aware that getting the most from a vendor's service is part-dependent on your being a good client and providing the vendors with the payments and other requested information in a timely manner.

Photography

★ 12 MONTHS PLUS

So much time, money, and emotion is spent planning your wedding day, it is important to hire the best photographer you can afford. No other vendor will have as lasting a role in your wedding as your wedding photographer; you will not begrudge this expense.

There are two basic styles of wedding photography, the photojournalistic approach and the traditional approach. Within each of these categories, there is scope for the photographer to utilize his/her talents and showcase his/her artistic expression.

The photojournalistic photographer shoots the day as if it were a news event, documenting and capturing the moments as they happen. The emphasis is on recording the pure emotion and action, with little posing. This type of photographer tries to be as unobtrusive as possible. The photographer should also offer you the option of some traditional shots to round out the day's coverage.

The traditional wedding photographer takes a more formal approach, utilizing more posing, lighting, and setting up shots to capture the images of the day. This is a photographer who will take the time to make sure that everything is posed perfectly for your special shots. He/she will take table shots and closely follow a shot list, to ensure you get all the posed shots that you expect.

Wedding Vendors

SERVICE	DATE BOOKED	DEPOSIT	FINAL PAYMENT	PAPERWORK
BRIDAL BEAUTY				
HAIR				
MAKEUP				
CATERER				
CAPPUCCINO SERVICE/COFFEE CART				
DANCE LESSONS				
ENTERTAINMENT				
CEREMONY				
COCKTAIL HOUR				
RECEPTION				
FLORAL DESIGNER				
INVITATIONS/STATIONERY				
LIGHTING				
OFFICIANT				
PHOTOGRAPHER				
RENTALS				
BASIC EQUIPMENT				
SPECIALTY LINENS				
SPECIALTY DECOR				
TRANSPORTATION				
BRIDE AND GROOM				
GUESTS				
PARENTS				
WEDDING PARTY				
VIDEOGRAPHER				
WEDDING CAKE/PASTRY CHEF				
WEDDING PLANNER				

Optional Extras

In addition to the wedding-day coverage, you may also want to ask the photographer about "extra" services:

💗 Engagement photo session: during this session, you, your fiancé, and the photographer spend an hour or so together. Apart from posed shots, it is a chance for you to get to know how the photographer works—and for him to get to know you as a couple. This means you are more likely to be relaxed in his presence on the wedding day. The session can take place soon after you hire the photographer so that you may include the photograph in your newspaper engagement announcement or on Save-the-Date cards and other wedding-related items. Photographers often include this session as part of their packages.

💗 Bridal portrait: this session allows the bride to dress in her full bridal ensemble and have formal posed portrait shots taken in the photographer's studio. Many brides choose this for use in the wedding announcement in the newspaper, though the option is less common than it once was.

💗 Parents' albums: these are smaller versions of the wedding album prepared specifically for the parents. They typically include family photos, photos of the bride/groom and her/his parents, and traditional wedding photos.

💗 Art prints: printing your wedding portraits on canvas or watercolor papers is quite popular. Photos printed on photographic paper can also be hand tinted and digitally enhanced.

💗 Other events: consider asking your photographer to attend one of your pre-wedding parties for some great informal photo opportunities.

Ask your photographer to attend a pre-wedding party for some great informal photos

INTERVIEWING PHOTOGRAPHERS When you meet with photographers, ask to see at least two complete wedding albums. Look for elements such as good composition, clearly focused photos, and proper lighting. You should take their personality into account because they will be around you on your wedding day.

Questions to Ask

💗 Describe your style? What is your specialty?

💗 What is your price range?

💗 Do you have a package or do you charge hourly?

💗 Is an engagement portrait included?

💗 How many hours are included?

💗 Who will shoot my wedding? May I meet with that photographer and see samples of their work?

💗 How many photographers and assistants will be there?

💗 What is the backup plan for equipment? Illness?

💗 Approximately how many photographs will be taken?

💗 Are proofs included? May we purchase them if not?

💗 Are negatives included? May we purchase them if not?

💗 Is an album included? May I see some samples?

💗 Is travel, setup, and strike time included?

💗 Do you shoot color and/or black and white? What about sepia prints? And digital images? Do you utilize special lenses?

💗 Do you/will you post our proofs on the Internet?

💗 Will you work to our shot list?

CONTRACTING A PHOTOGRAPHER Once you have selected a photographer, complete a detailed contract and pay your deposit. Make sure the contract includes:

💗 Date

💗 Times (of arrival and scheduled end time)

💗 All locations you expect the photographer to cover

💗 Name of photographer on the wedding day

💗 Complete price (including number of hours, photos, and albums included)

💗 Overtime fee

💗 Type of coverage (color, black and white, sepia, digital, 35mm, medium format)

💗 Delivery dates (negatives and/or proofs, and albums)

💗 Special requests

💗 Cancellation and postponement policy

AFTER THE WEDDING Two to four weeks after the wedding, your photographer will present you with "proofs" from the wedding day. The proofs are not retouched or cropped to perfection, but are the photographs you will use to determine the design and layout of the wedding album. The proofs that you see are typically not yours to keep; they often have copyright marks or numbers printed on them. Some photographers also publish your wedding photos on their websites, which makes it very easy for your friends, family, and guests to see the photos, too. Once you have reviewed your proofs and selected your favorites, you will work with your photographer to create the perfect layout for the album. Ask the photographer to confirm when you can expect to see the completed version.

Photographer

COMPANY:

CONTACT:

PHONE:

EMAIL:

FAX:

DEPOSIT:

FINAL PAYMENT DUE:

DETAILS:

SPECIAL INSTRUCTIONS:

Videography/Cinematography
★ 12 MONTHS PLUS

Like a photojournalistic photographer, the wedding videographer/cinematographer is there to capture the happenings of the day. His/her camera is there to record the live action, the vows you exchange, and the well wishes from guests. Many couples forgo having their wedding day filmed due to budgetary constraints or because they simply do not want more cameras pointed at them. One thing is certain, putting your wedding day on video or film will ensure you have a lasting record to show future generations.

Videography may have a reputation for cheesy guest interviews and canned comments, which is not wholly deserved. Forward-thinking wedding cinematographers— as many now like to be called — are shooting in more documentary style (think photojournalistic photography) and even real film, rather than on video, giving the recording a stylized feel. Such improvements make it hard for brides to say no to filming their wedding day.

One of the most important aspects of filming the wedding day is the technical ability of the person behind the camera and his ability to edit the film into a cohesive and romantic story of the day. Favorite songs, childhood recordings, old photos, and recorded messages from the couple as well as close friends and family can be incorporated into the final product. Editing time, though, is costly; a more budget-friendly option is to purchase raw footage of your wedding day, or to have only your ceremony recorded.

Putting your wedding day on film ensures you have a record to show future generations

**INTERVIEWING VIDEOGRAPHERS/
CINEMATOGRAPHERS** As with photographers, when
you meet with videographers/cinematographers, ask to see
not only a highlight or compilation sample of their work
but also at least two complete edited samples (a recording
from beginning to end). Once again, look for elements
such as good composition, clearly focused shots, and
proper lighting. And remember the videographer/
cinematographer will be with you for the entire day, so
take his/her personality into account. When interviewing,
you need to ask similar questions as of a photographer:

Questions to Ask

- Describe your style? What is your specialty?
- What is your price range (packages begin at what price)?
- Do you have a package or do you charge hourly?
- How many hours of labor are included on the wedding day?
- Who will shoot my wedding (if it is a large studio)? May I meet with that videographer? May I see samples of that person's work?
- How many videographers will be there on my wedding day? Assistants?
- What is the backup plan for equipment? In case of illness?
- How many hours of raw footage do you shoot?
- How long is the final edited version of the film?
- How many DVDs are included?
- Is travel, setup, and strike time included?
- What format do you shoot in: video, film, digital?
- How long does it take to edit the final version?

Videography/Cinematography

COMPANY:

CONTACT:

PHONE:

EMAIL:

FAX:

DEPOSIT:

FINAL PAYMENT DUE:

DETAILS:

SPECIAL INSTRUCTIONS:

**CONTRACTING A VIDEOGRAPHER/
CINEMATOGRAPHER** Once you have selected
a videographer/cinematographer, complete a detailed
contract and pay your deposit (usually half the full
contracted amount). Include the specifics on the
contract, such as:

- ♥ Date
- ♥ Times (of arrival and scheduled end time)
- ♥ All locations where you expect the videographer/
  cinematographer to shoot (for example, the parent's
  house or hotel for getting ready, venue for ceremony,
  reception)
- ♥ Name of videographer/cinematographer on the
  wedding day
- ♥ Complete price (including number of hours on
  the wedding day, number of hours of raw footage,
  and number of DVDs included)
- ♥ Overtime fees
- ♥ Type of coverage (video, film, digital video)
- ♥ Length/time of edited wedding recording
- ♥ Delivery dates
- ♥ Editing features or effects
- ♥ Special requests
- ♥ Cancellation and postponement policy

AFTER THE WEDDING Delivery time of your final
edited product depends on the number of copies you
order, the number of special effects or specialized
interviews you want to add, and the amount of editing
needed to complete the recording. If you plan to add
special music or family photos, the completion time will
also be determined by how promptly you can deliver these
items to the videographer/cinematographer (you can
compile these items prior to the wedding day for faster
turnaround time). Discuss these issues with the
videographer/cinematographer when completing the
contract and have them add an approximate completion
date to the contract.

The Ceremony

♥ Hiring an Officiant

♥ Planning the Ceremony

♥ Choosing Ceremony Music

♥ Choosing Wedding Bands

♥ Choosing Transportation

♥ The Marriage License

♥ The Ceremony Processional

♥ Rituals and Customs from Around the Globe

A wedding is truly about the ceremony. For all the spectacle, this is the important bit. You are surrounded by family and friends who are here to witness your official and legal union, as well as to celebrate your love for one another. This chapter covers planning the ceremony as well as obtaining a license, choosing vows, bands, readings, blessings and other beautiful wedding traditions.

Hiring an Officiant

★ EIGHT TO TEN MONTHS

If you have chosen to marry at a non-religious location, you will need to hire an Officiant. The Officiant should represent and reflect your feelings and beliefs. This can be a judge, a non-denominational minister, possibly the Officiant from your regular house of worship, and in some counties your friends and families can be deputized for a day to marry you. Most importantly, the Officiant must be legally certified to marry you in the county/state/country.

When planning the ceremony, he/she should be able to provide you with ideas and direction for creating the ceremony. There are numerous spiritual, wedding-related publications and online sources to help with this also. The Officiant you hire for your wedding ceremony should be willing to assist with organizing the ceremony and creating a ceremony to please you and your families.

Questions to Ask

♥ Do you specialize in a type of ceremony—are you more religious or spiritual?

♥ May we see some samples of ceremonies you have created?

♥ What is your attire on the day?

♥ Are you legally qualified to marry us in (insert county/state)?

♥ Do you have any restrictions on the type of events/readings/music we select for the ceremony?

♥ Are we required to take premarital counseling or classes?

♥ How long is the ceremony and what is included in the ceremony?

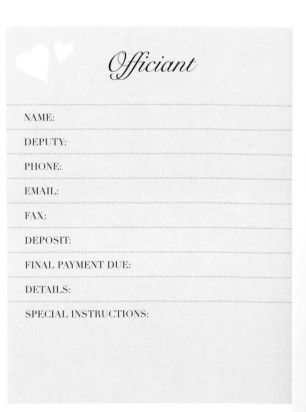

Officiant

NAME:

DEPUTY:

PHONE:

EMAIL:

FAX:

DEPOSIT:

FINAL PAYMENT DUE:

DETAILS:

SPECIAL INSTRUCTIONS:

Planning the Ceremony

★ SIX TO EIGHT MONTHS

There are many ways to personalize and create a beautiful wedding ceremony. In addition to the traditional, non-denominational items listed here, there are also cultural, religious, and ethnic traditions that may be incorporated into the ceremony (see page 117). Incorporating your personalities and family traditions, when possible, is also a great way to personalize the ceremony. The following outline is a basic order of events that apply to most ceremonies, whether they are held in a house of worship or a non-religious location.

Outline of Ceremony

The wedding ceremony may include the following components, though not all may be relevant to your wedding ceremony:

- ♥ Seating of the guests: music is played. As guests arrive, the ushers escort them to their seats.
- ♥ Seating of the families: after the guests are seated, this signifies the beginning of the formal ceremony. First the groom's parents are escorted to their seats. Then, the bride's mother is escorted to her seat while the bride's father remains with the bride. If grandparents are included they are seated prior to the parents.
- ♥ The groom and men enter: the Officiant, groom, best man, and groomsmen enter the ceremony. Groomsmen may escort the bridesmaids down the aisle.

- ♥ Processional: the bridesmaids (and possibly groomsmen), ring bearer, and flower girls proceed down the aisle and take their positions.
- ♥ Entrance of the bride: the bride enters, escorted by her father, mother, or both parents.
- ♥ Declaration of intent: do you take this man/woman to be your husband/wife?
- ♥ Exchange of vows: traditional wedding vows are always popular, but you may want to consider writing your own vows. You will need to discuss this option with your ceremony coordinator and Officiant for approval. Inspiration for your vows could come from love letters, favorite poems, even song lyrics. There are also books available with sample ceremonies and vows.
- ♥ Exchange of rings: the couple exchange the wedding bands.
- ♥ Scriptural readings: anywhere from one to three readings may be part of a ceremony. In a church setting these readings are scriptural readings about love, marriage, joy, and happiness, usually selected from an approved list provided by the location.
- ♥ Non-scriptural readings: in non-religious settings, poems, love letters, verses from love songs, original writings, or passages from favorite books may be read during the ceremony. The readers are usually close friends or relatives.
- ♥ Musical selection: in religious settings, the music usually has to be religious in nature, but in non-religious settings there is greater freedom in choosing music. You can select favorite contemporary tunes to walk up or down the aisle.
- ♥ Solos: a solo performance by either a professional or a talented friend/relative can usually be incorporated into the ceremony format.
- ♥ Introductions: the Officiant introduces the couple for the first time as husband and wife.
- ♥ Recessional: The couple, followed by the wedding party, and finally the parents, exits the ceremony location. The guests exit after this.

Incorporating your family traditions is a great way to personalize the ceremony

Choosing Ceremony Music

If you are marrying in a house of worship, the venue will most likely offer ceremony musicians (organist, soloist) for you to hire at a minimal cost. Of course, pending the venue's approval, you may be able to hire outside musicians, say a string quartet or a traditional classical ensemble, to play during the ceremony. The venue will also provide you with a list of music pieces to choose from; the selections will (almost always) need to be religious in nature.

If you are marrying elsewhere, you have more flexibility in your selection of musicians and musical pieces to play for the ceremony. You can play recorded music or hire a group to play for you. The choice of music can also be more personalized – walk down the aisle to "your song" and recess to your college alumna mater if you want. While string quartets are always appropriate, jazz trios and vocalists lend an original tone to the day.

When you select your ceremony musicians, sign a contract that details the following:

- Size and style of the group (include instruments and specific musicians or vocalists if these details are important to you).
- Start time of the pre-ceremony music, the ceremony itself, and how long you would like the musicians to play after the ceremony.
- Fees and overtime rates.
- Special requests you have, such as learning a new piece of music or song for your wedding, and whether this entails an additional cost.
- Special requests/needs for the musicians (area required, number of chairs, whether they need to be located in shade if the ceremony is outdoors, accessibility for a large instrument like a harp, electrical supply).
- Attire for the wedding.

Choosing Wedding Bands

⭐ FOUR TO SIX MONTHS

A wedding band is a sentimental and meaningful reminder of your love and marriage. It is a piece of jewelry you will be wearing for the rest of your life. So take time to think about what styles and options will work for both you and your fiancé. Shop at a trusted jeweler, such as the one where your engagement ring was purchased.

Matching your Style

Often the style of a bride's engagement ring determines the style of her wedding band, as they are traditionally worn together (the wedding band goes on first). The groom has more leeway in determining his style, but often chooses to select a band that complements the bride's, utilizing the same type of metal. Lifestyle may also dictate the style of ring—is a diamond eternity band too flashy? Do you work with your hands a lot? If so, you may want to avoid sharp edges. When in doubt, you can never go wrong with classic bands in gold or platinum.

Wedding Band Jeweler

COMPANY/STORE:

CONTACT:

PHONE:

EMAIL:

DATE ORDERED/DEPOSIT:

DATE EXPECTED/FINAL PAYMENT:

INSCRIPTIONS:

Choosing Transportation

Transportation for the bride and groom, wedding party, and families is an important factor on the wedding day. You will need to ensure these key players have transportation to and from the getting-ready location, to the ceremony, from the ceremony to the reception, and from the reception back to their hotel/home/car.

Arranging transport can be as easy as asking groomsmen, ushers, or helpful friends who are familiar with the location of the wedding to carpool/caravan with others in the wedding party. More often, however, couples choose to arrange for chauffered transportation, not least because it leaves your guests free to drink alcohol. Luxury coaches that can hold the entire wedding party, limousines, and town cars are popular options. Many transportation companies also offer extravagant options such as Mercedes, Navigator, and Hummer limousines.

You and your fiancé may wish to arrange for very special transportation for the two of you after the ceremony or reception. Do you dream of arriving for the ceremony in a horse-drawn carriage? Does your fiancé have visions of driving you into the sunset in a Ferrari? The options for coming and going are limitless.

Making an Entrance

Depending on the style of your gown, you may wish to keep things traditional for the arrival at the ceremony, and be a little more daring for your exit.

Once you have determined the mode of transportation, sign a contract that includes the following:

- Color of car (if applicable)
- Drop off times and locations
- Make and model of car (if applicable)
- Overtime fees and gratuities
- Passenger names (if possible/necessary)
- Pick up times and locations
- Special requests (do you want a particular brand of champagne awaiting you in the limousine?)
- Special directions

111

The Marriage License

★ RESEARCH THREE MONTHS/
OBTAIN ONE MONTH

Every couple must have a marriage license to make their union official and legal. Don't be caught off guard—early on, you must verify the marriage requirements of the city, county, or state in which you will be holding the ceremony. Since regulations vary from state to state and from county to county, contact the county clerk's office to check on the requirements.

In most cases, you and your fiancé will need to apply together in person and be able to provide identification and proof of age. Additionally, you will need to know/confirm the following:

- ♥ What is the fee? What forms of payment are accepted?
- ♥ Is there a waiting period?
- ♥ How long is the license valid (usually 30 days)?
- ♥ Must you provide proof of divorce?
- ♥ Do we need a blood test?
- ♥ If underage, what form of parental consent is needed?

Marrying Abroad

If you are planning to marry abroad (or even in your hometown if you no longer live there), you must verify the legalities of obtaining a marriage certificate and making your union legal. Depending on the location, you will need to contact the country's embassy, consulate, or department of tourism for direction and assistance in this process. If you are working with a resort to plan your destination wedding or with a wedding planner in the country/locale, they should also be able to provide assistance. A quick search on the Internet may also provide you with the information you need. However, always call the appropriate agency to confirm that the information you find is correct and current.

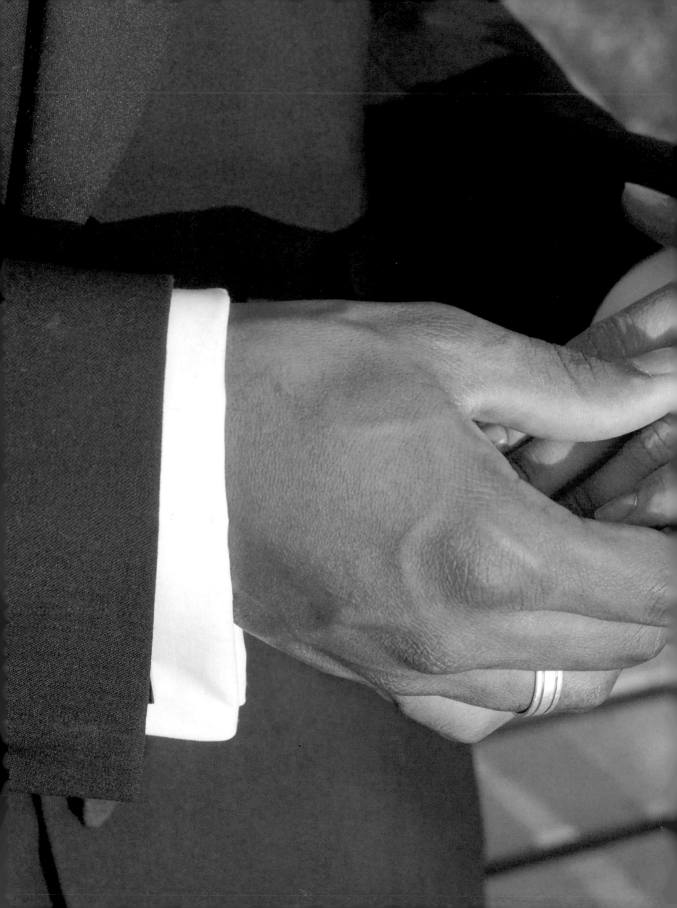

The Ceremony Processional

A traditional ceremony processional is configured as follows, although there are many variations. Your wedding planner, church coordinator, or Officiant will be able to provide guidance for your situation. The recessional is the reverse order, with bridesmaids and groomsmen paired up.

Traditional Line Up
FORMALLY SEATED:
- 💜 Grandparents (optional) beginning with groom's grandparents followed by bride's grandparents
- 💜 Groom's mother (by groomsman but can also be seated by groom)
- 💜 Bride's mother (by groomsman)

ENTER:
- 💜 Officiant
- 💜 Groom
- 💜 Best man

PROCESS DOWN AISLE:
- 💜 Junior bridesmaids and junior groomsmen in pairs
- 💜 Bridesmaids and groomsmen in pairs
- 💜 Maid/matron of honor
- 💜 Ring bearer(s)
- 💜 Flower girl(s)
- 💜 Bride and her escort (usually her father, but may include mother, too)
- 💜 Page/train bearers following bride and carrying her train

In England, the bride sometimes carries a horseshoe as a sign of good luck

Rituals and Customs from Around the Globe

Different cultures and religions include symbolic and meaningful exchanges to signify and seal the bond of marriage. Borrowing elements and taking cues from other cultures and religions can inspire you to create a unique and meaningful ceremony.

Wedding Customs

❤ In a Jewish processional, both parents escort their children down the aisle. This emphasizes the role of both parents leading their children through life, and demonstrates the uniting of the families.

❤ It is a Belgian custom for the bride to give her mother a rose on the way down the aisle, and then after the declaration of marriage the bride and groom together present the groom's mother with a rose. This ceremony symbolizes the two families becoming one. At the conclusion of the ceremony (just prior to the recessional), the groom will present a rose to the bride's mother, and the bride will present a rose to the groom's mother.

❤ In England, the bride sometimes carries a horseshoe as a sign of good luck.

❤ In Latin cultures, the lasso symbolizes unity. It is often made of flowers or orange blossoms (representing fertility) or of rosary beads. After the exchange of rings, persons close to the couple place the lasso around the shoulders of the newly weds.

❤ In India, the siblings of the bride and groom toss petals at the newly married couple to ward off evil spirits and to bring good luck.

❤ It is a Czech custom for the bridesmaids to pin rosemary to the guests as a symbol of fertility.

❤ The Caim is a Celtic custom that symbolizes unity with God. A garland of petals is placed around the bride and groom while the Caim Prayer is recited.

❤ In a Hindu wedding, the bride and groom meet before the wedding platform to exchange floral garlands, which are then worn throughout the ceremony.

❤ A French custom is to toss laurel leaves at the bride and groom (instead of rice or birdseed).

❤ The Unity Candle is a popular wedding ritual. The mothers of the bride and groom come forward and each lights a candle. Later in the ceremony, the bride and groom use those candles to simultaneously light one larger "unity" candle together.

❤ Hawaiian ceremonies use the exchanging of garlands (leis) to seal the union at the end of the ceremony, before they recess down the aisle.

❤ The Chinese tea ceremony is the traditional final duty of the bride on her wedding day. In a room, a table is set with symbolic offerings. In Japan, the bride performs a similar ceremony with sake.

The Reception

13

- ♥ Planning the Reception

- ♥ Menu Planning

- ♥ Parking

- ♥ Entertainment/Emcee

- ♥ Seating Plan

- ♥ Guest Book

This is where the fun begins. Brides and grooms are getting truly creative with their wedding reception ideas, but at the heart of all the excitement and exuberance should lie a solid timeline, good food, and good entertainment. Your guests will appreciate the time and effort you put into planning the reception and all the details that make it a truly memorable party.

Planning the Reception

★ SIX TO EIGHT MONTHS

The wedding reception is possibly the biggest party of your life. After saying "I do," it is time to relax, enjoy, and start your married life surrounded by well wishing family and friends. Before you get to that point, there is a lot of planning to do.

The components of a wedding reception may include the following elements:

♥ Cocktail hour: this is held when guests arrive at the venue so that they can enjoy drinks and hors d'oeuvres while the bride, groom, and wedding party finish their formal photography session.

♥ Receiving line: a receiving line is set up prior to the guests entering the dining area. The bride, groom, and their families (and sometimes the wedding party) greet the guests as they enter the reception. (If you choose not to do this, make your way around each guest table to say hello and thank your guests for attending.)

♥ Grand entrance: this is the first introduction of the bride and groom at the reception. It is done as soon as the guests are seated in the main reception/dining room. Traditionally, the bride and groom as well as the entire wedding party (and sometimes parents) are formally announced into the reception. The current trend is to introduce only the bride and groom.

♥ Toasts: the best man's toast is traditionally the first one. It usually takes place toward the beginning of the reception—following the grand entrance or before/after the first course. The maid of honor often proposes a toast as well. The father of the bride may also start off by welcoming the guests and concluding with a toast to the bride and groom. Finally, the groom may also wish to toast his bride and thank her family, and of course the bride may make a toast as well. If there are many toasts, spread them throughout the evening leaving the best man to start things off.

♥ Protocol dances: the bride and groom's first dance is traditionally the first dance of the evening. It may be done immediately following the grand entrance, between courses, or after the meal. Once the first dance has been danced, the floor is "officially" open to the other guests. A father/daughter dance, where the bride and her father take the dance floor for a song is expected. The groom and his mother will often join in halfway through the song. A wedding party dance or a family dance may also be done.

♥ Cake cutting: the cake cutting is often done later in the evening, an hour or so after the meal service concludes. During the official cake cutting, the bride and groom cut the cake together and feed each other a bite of cake. Cake may be packed in small boxes and distributed to guests as they leave.

♥ Bouquet and garter toss: toward the end of the evening the bride tosses the bouquet, and then the groom removes the garter from the bride's leg and tosses that as well. Tradition says that those who catch these items will be the next to be married. The bouquet can also be tossed as the couple leaves the reception.

♥ Last dance or grand exit: for a last dance, the guests join the bride and groom on the dance floor for the last song of the evening. For a grand exit, the bride and groom "run" to the car or other vehicle through a pathway lined by the guests. They are then whisked away to their wedding night destination.

Dance Lessons

⭐ **SIX TO EIGHT MONTHS**

One surefire way to start your reception off with pizzazz is for you and your fiancé to learn a special dance for your first dance as a married couple. Twirling round the dance floor to a choreographed routine will wow the guests and add a touch of sparkle and sophistication to your reception. If you decide to take dance lessons, begin your lessons at least six months prior to the wedding date so that you have plenty of time to practice. Also, consult with your teacher so that you have the proper shoes (you may need to change from your wedding shoes). You can find dance instructors through referrals, wedding websites, and in the phone book.

Menu Planning

In addition to determining which reception events and protocol you wish to follow, you must also select a menu for your meal and beverage service. Typically you will be selecting hors d'oeuvres for the cocktail hour, the meal itself, and possibly a dessert. You also need to decide what beverage and/or bar service you will offer the guests.

Meal Service

Here you have a few options. The first is the sit-down or plated meal. This is a more formal meal service, which usually involves three courses, a salad/soup/appetizer, an entrée, and a dessert. Other combinations include a salad/soup/appetizer, an intermezzo, and an entrée. Of course many upscale locations offer four- and five-course meals as well. It is important to make sure the venue/caterer has enough wait staff to serve all the guests in a timely fashion.

A second option in which guests are served at their table is known as "family style." Family style meals are now increasingly served at both formal and casual weddings. The caterer serves the dishes to the tables and the guests pass them around, serving themselves as if they were at your home.

A third option is the buffet, which is frequently associated with more casual affairs. Here the buffet offers a display of food that guests can revisit as often as they like. Buffets may be self-service or the food may be served by wait staff standing at the buffet table. For buffets, make sure there are enough clean plates for multiple visits through the line, that the catering manager or emcee of the evening has a system for sending guests to the buffet to avoid long lines, and finally, if it is a large wedding, that there are two or more buffet lines set up to avoid bottlenecks.

A variation of the buffet is to set up food stations. Food stations are one of the most popular options, offering guests made-to-order dishes. Typically there are three stations around the venue, each offering specialties (sushi stations, pasta stations, salad stations, for example). Because you require chefs on hand at each of the stations, this is one of the more costly options.

Beverage or Bar Service

There is no obligation to serve alcohol at a wedding reception, just the obligation to provide guests with beverages (the guests would not expect to pay for drinks straight after the ceremony). You need to determine the type of beverage service—for example, a non-alcoholic bar, a wine and champagne bar, or a full bar. You also need to decide whether or not to have wine served at the table, and whether the traditional toast will be made with champagne or sparkling wine. Finally, many couples are choosing to serve a specialty drink at their wedding, either one that follows the theme of the day or simply a drink that is special to the bride and groom.

Parking

⭐ SIX TO EIGHT MONTHS

Some locations require valet parking due to space restrictions or basic policy. Others may have self-parking, and still others (like off-premise venues) may require the rental of a nearby parking lot with shuttles to and from the site. Whatever your location requires, it is up to you to make arrangements that will be the most convenient for the guests and, as hosts of the party, you should be paying for the parking and gratuities, not the guests.

Valet Parking/ Shuttle Company

COMPANY:

CONTACT:

PHONE:

EMAIL:

FAX:

DEPOSIT:

FINAL PAYMENT:

SPECIAL INSTRUCTIONS:

The Reception

Make arrangements that will be convenient for your guests

Entertainment/Emcee

★ TEN TO TWELVE MONTHS

A good Disc Jockey (DJ) or band is an essential element for the wedding reception and can make or break the "party." The DJ or bandleader also typically acts as emcee for the event, making announcements and leading the bride, groom, and guests through the reception. As a rule, bands cost more than DJs, but ultimately it comes down to the couple's preference for recorded or live music. These days, many budget-conscious couples are buying individual songs for their portable music players and asking their friends to emcee.

You will work closely with your DJ or bandleader to develop a timeline and order of reception events. You will also work with him or her to select special songs to be played throughout the event (they will provide you with worksheets to assist in completing this task). As with other wedding vendors, be sure you like this person, his/her personality, and presentation because all of your guests will be seeing and listening to him/her as well as you. When interviewing entertainment vendors, ask for reference letters and possibly to view videotape of them "in action."

Questions to Ask

💗 What is the band's specialty/forte? Do you specialize in rock & roll, jazz, or blues? (For DJ) Do you specialize in a certain style or sound or genre of music?

💗 How many members are in the band? (For a DJ) Do you work alone or with an assistant?

💗 What is your attire for the event?

💗 What equipment do you bring? Do you have a song list we must select from, or are you willing to learn/find special requests?

💗 What are the fees? How many hours does that include? Is overtime available? At what cost?

💗 How many breaks do you require during a typical four- or five-hour reception?

Entertainment

COMPANY:

CONTACT:

PHONE:

EMAIL:

FAX:

DEPOSIT:

FINAL PAYMENT:

SPECIAL INSTRUCTIONS:

DETAILS:

Seating Plan

★ TWO TO FOUR WEEKS

A seating plan provides guests with direction at the reception and alleviates feelings of awkwardness that some may feel as they search for an open seat. Begin the seating plan as soon as the responses to your invitations come in, and enlist the assistance of the groom and your families with this task. Work with your reception location to finalize a floor plan and table arrangements for the dining room. The reception location should be able to provide you with a basic floor plan that outlines the placement of the room (such as the dance floor, bar, guest book, and gift table.) Ask the reception location how many guests may be seated at each table (usually eight to ten persons per 60-inch round table). This will determine the number of tables you will need for dining.

You will need escort cards to inform guests of their table arrangements. If you choose to also "assign" places at each table, you will need place cards, too. You (and a few bridesmaids) can be responsible for printing the escort/place cards or look into hiring a calligrapher to complete them. Some couples choose to make large framed charts and display them on easels at the reception in lieu of escort cards.

Guest Book

A guest book is a record of the names and well wishes of guests who attend your wedding celebration. Traditionally, the guest book is offered for signing at the church, but many couples also choose to offer it at the reception for those who missed signing it at the church. An attendant is often selected to oversee the signing of the book.

Once a simply adorned book with decorative pen, the guest book now takes on many creative forms. As many of the following options are a little more complicated and take more time to execute than a traditional guest book, it is best to bring them out only at the reception. This way, the ceremony will not be delayed and guests will have time throughout the evening to enjoy this task and really be creative.

♥ An engagement photo "framed" by a large blank photo matte where the guests can sign all around the matte and then after the wedding the couple can complete the framing process and hang it on the wall of their home.

♥ Instant photo scrapbooks where the guests snap photos with a Polaroid camera or in a vintage photo booth and then place their photos in a scrapbook and write the couple a note next to the photo.

♥ Blank art books, where the guests are invited to partake in drawing, coloring, and composing all sorts of creative messages. Provide crayons and pens and let the guests have fun.

♥ A silver tray that guests can sign with an engraving pen will provide a lasting memento. It will take some time for guests to sign and you will need to have someone available to assist the guests.

Give guests time to enjoy writing their messages and to really be creative

Final Preparations

14

- ♥ Prepare a Wedding-Day Timeline
- ♥ Finalize and Confirm the Details
- ♥ The Ceremony Rehearsal
- ♥ Review Attire
- ♥ Wedding Accessories
- ♥ Prepare an Emergency Kit

The final weeks leading up to the actual wedding day are fun and terribly hectic. They can also be the most stressful for the bride, anxious to ensure all the details are attended to and finalized. Unless you are working with a wedding planner, creating a wedding-day timeline rests on your shoulders. Being prepared with a good plan will help to prevent you and your fiancé feeling overwhelmed.

Prepare a Wedding-Day Timeline

★ FOUR TO SIX MONTHS

A wedding-day timeline should include a complete schedule for the wedding day, beginning with the bride preparing for the day and ending with the couple's departure from the reception. It answers all the important questions: Who will walk down the aisle? Who will make the first toast? What is the first dance song? Who will take the gifts home?

Some couples choose to leave the timing of the wedding ceremony to the venue, and let the catering manager and entertainment/emcee lead the timing of the reception. However, you can take a more proactive approach and, working with your vendors and venue managers, create a personalized wedding-day timeline to ensure it unfolds exactly as you imagined. If you want to be actively involved and stay on track, these are the main steps to create a wedding-day timeline:

💗 Start with the established start times of the ceremony and reception and use them to work forward and backward to fill in the remaining portions of the schedule. Ask at the ceremony and/or reception venues about set-up and arrival times.

💗 Take into account travel time between locations.

💗 Schedule the pre-ceremony activities.

💗 Confirm all times. Double-check with the venues and vendors on their timing. Ask the catering manager to confirm that the key timing points for formalities will work with the times for meal service.

💗 Schedule photography time. Heed the photographer's advice when scheduling.

💗 Gather contact names, office phone numbers, and pager or cell phone numbers for all of your vendors, and record this information on the timeline so that it is all easily available.

💗 Know which formalities and protocols you wish to incorporate.

💗 Include specifics such as titles of selected songs, names of those proposing toasts, and so on.

💗 Know vendor arrival and departure times. Check that the order and times make sense. For example, if the first photos are to be at the bride's parents' home, you want the florist to deliver the bouquets to the home and not the ceremony venue. Make sure the florist decorates the ceremony venue before going to the reception location.

💗 Include the details, for example linen colors, table favor placement, where accessories are to be placed, and the number of candles on each dining table.

Finalize and Confirm the Details

As the wedding day draws nearer, it is important to check in with your vendors and provide each one with a copy of the completed wedding-day timeline. Fax or email the timeline to all vendors and call each vendor afterward to confirm it has been received, go over specific details, and answer any questions they may have. Include directions to the wedding locations with this timeline. Also, be sure to make enough photocopies of the itinerary to distribute to the families and wedding party at the rehearsal. For the wedding party, it is a good idea to include directions to the rehearsal dinner on the back of the itinerary.

Create a personalized timeline to ensure the day unfolds just as you imagined

The Ceremony Rehearsal

The ceremony rehearsal generally takes place one to two days prior to the ceremony. Everyone who has a role in the ceremony is expected to attend. If you are marrying in a house of worship, chances are very good the venue's on-site wedding coordinator will be running the rehearsal, so if you have done your ceremony preparations, you will not have much to do or to worry about. The coordinator will lead you and the family and wedding party through the ceremony rehearsal.

If you are marrying at an off-premise venue, hopefully the Officiant you hired will be attending the rehearsal and running it, but if you are running your own rehearsal, make a plan. Draw yourself a diagram of the processional and recessional (see page 116), and make your own rehearsal timeline. Start by showing the families and wedding party their places, practicing the recessional and processional, and going over timing for the day. If you have readers or soloists, plan them in too.

After the rehearsal, distribute the wedding-day timeline, answer any questions, and reiterate how important it is that each person has their wedding attire checked and ready for the wedding day. If possible, drop off any ceremony accessories to the venue, wedding planner, or a trusted friend to take to the venue on the wedding day. At the rehearsal, you may also want to give vendor payments and tips, the marriage license, and the wedding rings to the best man or maid/matron of honor.

Payments and Tips

Most vendors require final payment in full about 14 days prior to the wedding. Refer to the vendor checklist on page 95 to confirm which payments are due and when. A few vendors will require final payment on the wedding day, in which case, prepare envelopes with the appropriate amounts and give them to the wedding planner or best man to present to the vendor. Be sure to confirm what payment methods will be accepted.

In all cases, tipping is voluntary. If tipping is just not in your budget, a glowing thank you or reference letter is always appreciated. However, you may find that some vendors and locations expect tips—even outline them in their contracts. Gratuities should be given as an expression of gratitude when you have received excellent service. It is always a good idea to have some "extra" cash on hand in case you would like to increase a vendor's gratuity or to make up for any discrepancies.

The following is a list of those vendors who typically receive gratuities. The amounts cover a range of budgets. The level of service and location of the wedding (high end hotel = larger tips) may call for more than the amounts designated:

- Catering manager/site coordinator/food and beverage director: $50–$350+
- Banquet captain: A set amount, say $50–350+ or tip per person, $1–5 per guest
- Bellman: $5–25 each
- Florist/event design team: $50–250
- Wedding planner and assistants: $50–350+ or 10% of total bill
- Limousine driver: 15–20% of total bill
- Live musicians/DJ: $25–75 each for live musicians/$50–200+ for a DJ
- Makeup/hair stylists: 15–20% of total bill, or designated amount of $25–100 per stylist
- Parking attendants/coat room/powder room attendant: 50¢–$2 per guest or car is acceptable. As host, you may want to cover all tipping at the end of the reception.
- Videographers: $30–200
- Photographers: $30–200
- Rentals and delivery personnel: $10–30

Review Attire

Review and check everyone's attire early on to avoid last-minute panics:

For the Bride

♥ At the final dress fitting have your veil and headpiece, lingerie, shoes, and accessories for the wedding day purchased. Take them with you to the fitting and try on the complete ensemble.

♥ Make a checklist of these items for the wedding day as well as other items (such as deodorant, perfume, makeup) you must have when you dress on the day.

♥ When you collect your pressed gown from the dressmakers, avoid trying it on or touching it. Put it safely away until it is time to wear it, and follow any special instructions given to you by the dressmaker.

♥ Do not forget your "something old, something new, something borrowed, and something blue."

For the Groom, Groomsmen, Junior Groomsmen, Ring Bearers, Train Bearers, and Fathers

♥ When the suits/tuxedos are collected from the formalwear store or tailor, try on everything for fit and check you have everything you need: button covers, cufflinks, shoes, the pieces of the tuxedo (jacket, pants, suspenders, dress shirt, tie/bowtie, cummerbund or vest).

♥ Don't forget to have the men pack a white undershirt and black socks for the day. (You may want to make a master checklist of items to remember and email it to the men.)

♥ Rented formal shoes are notoriously uncomfortable, consider letting the men wear their own black dress shoes if they have them (no one will notice the difference).

For the Bridesmaids, Junior Bridesmaids, Flower Girls, and Mothers

♥ For the final fitting, make sure they have their appropriate lingerie, shoes, and accessories purchased so that they can take these items along for the fitting.

♥ Have the women make a checklist of these and other items (such as deodorant, perfume, makeup) they will need for the day. You may want to prepare a master checklist of items and email it to the women.

♥ Remind them that when they collect their dress to avoid trying it on or touching it and to follow any special instructions given to them by the dressmaker.

Do not forget your "something old, something new, something borrowed, something blue"

Wedding Accessories

There are many items—decorative, essential, and traditional—that you may want for the wedding day. Some you will need to purchase, but you may be able to borrow others from recently married friends. You may even be able to register for some of the items, like a cake knife and server and toasting flutes, on your Bridal Gift Registry.

Ceremony Accessories

- [ ] Ceremony programs
- [ ] Ring pillow(s)
- [ ] Guest book and pen
- [ ] Unity candle
- [ ] Cultural or religious symbols/items

Wedding Reception Accessories

- [ ] Cake knife and server
- [ ] Cake topper
- [ ] Card box (for gift table)
- [ ] Centerpieces
- [ ] Decorations
- [ ] Disposable table cameras
- [ ] Engagement photos
- [ ] Favors
- [ ] Guest book and pen
- [ ] Place cards
- [ ] Table numbers
- [ ] Toasting flutes

Prepare an Emergency Kit

You really never know what difficulties may arise on the wedding day. The items listed opposite are the basics to include in a wedding-day emergency kit. These items will allow you to do everything from cleaning a dress to sewing on a button to plugging in twinkle lights. If you are having an off-premise event or have very intricate decor planned, you may need to include additional items that would be specific to your site.

Emergency Kit

- [ ] Baby wipes
- [ ] Black pen
- [ ] Bobby pins
- [ ] Bottled water
- [ ] Chalk (white for gown touch up)
- [ ] Clear nail polish
- [ ] Clear tape
- [ ] Corsage pins
- [ ] Cotton swabs
- [ ] Deodorant (invisible)
- [ ] Duct tape
- [ ] Electrical cords
- [ ] Emery board
- [ ] Feminine products
- [ ] Hairspray
- [ ] Hot glue gun and glue sticks
- [ ] Masking tape
- [ ] Matches
- [ ] Mints
- [ ] Mouthwash
- [ ] Nail glue
- [ ] Pain reliever
- [ ] Protein bars and snacks
- [ ] Ribbon (to match ribbons you may have used in decor)
- [ ] Rubber bands
- [ ] Safety pins (large and small)
- [ ] Scissors
- [ ] Sewing kit (with thread to match bridesmaids', and groomsmen's attire)
- [ ] Sheer band aids
- [ ] Stain remover (preferably in wipe form)
- [ ] Spot remover and white cloth
- [ ] Static cling spray
- [ ] Talcum/baby powder
- [ ] Tissues
- [ ] Toothpaste/toothbrush
- [ ] Velcro (self stick)

After the Wedding

♥ Planning the Honeymoon

♥ Final Details

The party may be over, but there is so much to look forward to—and a few tasks to complete. The honeymoon is probably the most amazing vacation in a couple's life: and you've earned it! Included here are a few ideas for planning the trip, a packing checklist and a reminder of the few remaining items you need to cover to wrap up your wedding experience in style.

Planning the Honeymoon

★ SIX TO EIGHT MONTHS

The payoff for all of your hard work is the honeymoon. Whether your honeymoon is a few days at a local getaway or spending weeks on a tropical island, it is a romantic time for you and your (now) husband to relax, unwind, and enjoy being married. When you are planning your honeymoon, work with your fiancé to create a trip itinerary that will please the both of you. Each of you should make a list of possible destinations and activities you would like for your honeymoon and compare the two.

Travel agents and large resorts offer very enticing packages that are great ideas for the honeymoon. Work with an experienced travel agent or research on the Internet. Before putting down any deposits, check local travel warnings and seasonal weather warnings for the destination you select. Once you decide on a destination research and prepare any special travel documents. You may, for example, need a passport or any vaccines (your travel agent should be able to assist you with this information). Purchase a guidebook for the area and spend time at the library or online researching activities and special points of interest. You may even want to call the hotel where you will be staying to get suggestions an additional information on weather conditions and any other local information.

Ideas for making the honeymoon extra special:

♥ Arrive at the airport and/or hotel in style—book a limousine or town car.

♥ Ask about upgrading your airline tickets (unless you are already seated in first class).

♥ Call the hotel and arrange for champagne, chocolate candles, and fresh flowers to be awaiting you in you hotel room.

♥ Arrange for a romantic evening with a special cockt or dinner.

♥ Don't forget the lingerie!

Final Travel Plans and Accommodation

TRAVEL AGENT:

PHONE:

EMAIL:

DESTINATION:

TRAVEL DATES:

FLIGHT NUMBER:

AIRLINE:

800 NUMBER:

DEPARTURE TIME:

LODGING:

ADDRESS:

PHONE:

EMAIL:

CHECK IN TIME:

CHECK OUT TIME:

AMENITIES/SPECIAL PACKAGES:

Arrange to have champagne, chocolates, and fresh flowers to be awaiting you in your room

Preparing for the Trip

To prepare for this once-in-a-lifetime trip, you need to shop, pack, and make arrangements to keep your home, pets, and belongings safe while you are away.

Shopping List

- [ ] Clothing (appropriate for the trip—bathing suits or parkas, for example)
- [ ] Travel size toiletries
- [ ] Luggage, tags, and locks
- [ ] Travel hair dryer and curling irons
- [ ] Electrical adapters
- [ ] Camera (still, digital or video) and film (if necessary)
- [ ] Sporting gear (if applicable)
- [ ] Guidebooks for destination
- [ ] Lingerie
- [ ] Travel candles

Special Arrangements

- [ ] Get cash/foreign currency/traveler's checks
- [ ] Stop mail
- [ ] Hold shipments from gift registry
- [ ] Hire a house/pet sitter
- [ ] Other:

Final Details

Wedding Announcements

★ PLAN TWO TO SIX MONTHS PRIOR/
SEND OR PRINT FOLLOWING WEDDING

Printed wedding announcements are printed very much like a wedding invitation, except that the wording reflects the fact that the marriage has taken place. They should be mailed the day of, or immediately after, your wedding ceremony to distant relatives and friends who were not invited. Announcements should not be sent to those who attended or were invited to the ceremony and/or reception. There is no obligation to send announcements.

You may want to share the news of your nuptials in a newspaper announcement. The announcement can be published in the area you are currently living, where you grew up, and/or where your parents live. Your published announcement should be prepared about two months prior to the wedding date. The announcements are usually published within one to two months following the wedding. Call each publication to obtain their guidelines.

Preserving Your Bouquet

★ PLAN THREE MONTHS PRIOR

If you plan to preserve your bridal bouquet, you must research and book a company ahead of time. Preserving your flowers involves a chemical process to preserve the bouquet as it was on your wedding day. The bouquet must be delivered to the company within one to two days of the wedding—ask your maid/matron of honor to assist you with this task. Preservation companies will send you options for displaying your bouquet once it is preserved, a complete list of instructions, as well as a special box for transporting your bouquet.

Cleaning and Preserving Your Gown

★ PLAN THREE MONTHS PRIOR

The wedding gown holds tremendous sentimental value for some brides, and you may wish to have your gown professionally preserved to ensure its beauty for years to come. It is best to make plans for gown preservation prior to the wedding day (but it is not too late after, either). Ask a close friend, your mother, or maid/matron of honor to assist you with getting the gown to the preservation company while you are on your honeymoon. Note any stains on the gown and point them out to the company. The cleaned and preserved gown and veil should be wrapped in acid free paper and returned in a box that will protect it from light, insects, and acid.

Sending Thank-You Notes

★ ASAP

The task of writing thank-you notes may seem daunting but you must do it! Schedule a time to write thank-you notes as soon as possible after your return from the honeymoon. This task will be streamlined if you (or a relative or trusted friend) take proper care to carefully note who gave what when opening the gifts. Writing your thank-you notes right away ensures that the sweet memories of your wedding and the guests are fresh in your mind. A simple formula for writing thank-you notes is to mention the gift, note how you are going to use it,

...nd relay a personal comment about the guest's ...resence at the wedding. Remember to hand write the ...ote and that written appreciation is called for even if ...ou have expressed your gratitude verbally. A common ...isconception is that you have one year to write ...ank-you notes: this is not true—you should aim to ...omplete the task within two months.

Changing Your Name

★ AFTER THE WEDDING

...Whether or not you change your name is a personal ...ecision. There are various options: retain your maiden ...ame; hyphenate your maiden and married names; adopt ...our maiden name as a middle name and take your ...arried name as your last name; and keep your maiden ...ame strictly for business purposes (and use your married ...ame personally).

...o begin the process of changing your name, you can ...urchase ready-made "name change kits" on the Internet ... at bridal stores, call the appropriate office for forms, or ...se their website. Most agencies require official proof of ...e marriage, such as a certified marriage license with the ...ate seal, so you will need to wait for these documents ...ter the wedding.

...you change your name, some of the items/people you ...ll need to update include:

- Bank/investment/stock market accounts
- Business professionals (your lawyer, accountant, doctors)
- Car title/registration
- Credit cards
- Driver's license
- Insurance (car, homeowners, health)
- Internal Revenue Service
- Magazine/newspaper/professional subscriptions
- Memberships
- Passport
- Professional associations
- Property deeds
- Social security
- Utilities

Spreading the news of a name change (or retention) can be done in several ways:

- ♥ Your "thank you" or "at home" cards. Have the full names by which you and your husband will be known printed on the cards. For example: Mr. and Mrs. Joseph Smith (bride changing her name) or Ms. Jane Jones and Mr. Joseph Smith (bride keeping her maiden name).
- ♥ By using the appropriate names and titles in any marriage announcements published in a newspaper or other publication. You may wish to state, "Ms. Jane Jones will retain her maiden name" as part of the announcement.
- ♥ Be sure to update business associates if you are changing your name. Have a name card or formal announcement printed with your new name and mailed to business associates.

Index

Index

Acknowledgments

The publisher would like to thank the following for permission to reproduce copyright material:

Mark Lund/The Image Bank/Getty, page 2; Michael Goldman/Photographer's Choice/Getty, page 6; Steve Taylor/The Image Bank/Getty, page 10; Frank Herholdt/Taxi/Getty, page 11; Simon Marcus/Corbis, page 16; altrendo images/Getty, page 18; Robert Harding World Imagery/

Corbis, page 19; Jerome Corpuz/Stone/Getty, page 32; Guy Ryecart/Dorling Kindersley/Getty, page 47; David Lees/Taxi/Getty, page 48; Rick Rusing/Taxi/Getty, page 56; Francesca Yorke/StockFood Creative/Getty, page 76; Michael Goldman/Taxi/Getty, page 79; Jutta Klee/Taxi/Getty, page 80; photocuisine/Corbis, page 82; Jerry Driendl/Photographer's Choice/Getty, page 112; Steven Lam/Taxi/Getty, pages 113 and 117; Andy

Whale/Photonica/Getty, page 114; Hurewitz Creative/Corbis, page 124; Kevin Fitzgerald/Taxi/Getty, page 13 Michael Goldman/Photographer's Choice/Getty, page 141; and Grace/zefa/Corbis, front cover, top image.

Thank you to Clifton Photographic Company for their help in supplyin the remaining beautiful images and to all the wedding parties whose photographs are included.